PRAISE FOR

Healing: Bringing the Gift of God's Mercy to the World

Mary Healy, recently appointed a member of the Pontifical Biblical Commission, has written an extraordinary book on healing. Based on solid scholarship and extensive personal experience, and written in a very accessible style, my hope is that this book will stimulate conversation in the Church about this very important dimension of evangelization. And yet this book is written not just to give theoretical understanding but also to enable God's people to open themselves more fully to be used as instruments of healing and evangelization in the challenging times in which we are now living.

— Ralph Martin, founder and president
of Renewal Ministries

This is a timely book, especially for us who are increasingly pressured to privatize our faith. Not only does *Healing: Bringing the Gift of God's Mercy to the World* encourage us to live our faith boldly, but also to serve the Lord with gladness and to expect his mercy and his miracles to surround and sustain us. I strongly recommend Mary Healy's latest book.

— Most Rev. Thomas J. Olmsted,
bishop of Phoenix

In this skillfully written and inspirational book, Dr. Healy offers the whole Church an opportunity to contemplate God's desire to heal today. The book will inspire you with stories of the kingdom of God revealed through physical healing. You will receive refreshing insights into the New Testament accounts and an understanding of healing throughout Church history and its vital role today in the New Evangelization.

Healy not only calls for a restoration of healing ministry, she also shows us the way through her personal journey and practical instruction. A must read for anyone seriously examining the breadth and depth of the New Evangelization.

— Neal Lozano, founder and director
of Heart of the Father Ministries

Dr. Healy's book *Healing: Bringing the Gift of God's Mercy to the World* is challenging, instructive, and inspiring. It elevated my faith in God's faithfulness to confirm our proclamation of his gospel. As someone committed to equipping Catholics to evangelize, I believe this book is essential reading for anyone who is open to learning from Scripture, Tradition, and contemporary examples this important but neglected dimension of evangelization. *Healing: Bringing the Gift of God's Mercy to the World* opens us up to consider a radical paradigm shift that embraces the expectation of God's working with us to confirm the proclamation of the "word of his grace" with "signs and wonders" (Acts 14:3).

— Dave Nodar, founder and
director of ChristLife

Healing

Bringing the Gift of
God's Mercy to the World

Healing

Bringing the Gift of
God's Mercy to the World

MARY HEALY

Our Sunday Visitor Publishing Division
Our Sunday Visitor, Inc.
Huntington, Indiana 46750

Nihil Obstat:
Msgr. Michael Heintz, Ph.D.
Censor Librorum

Imprimatur:
✠ Kevin C. Rhoades
Bishop of Fort Wayne-South Bend
May 19, 2015

Our Sunday Visitor Publishing Division, Our Sunday Visitor, Inc., 200 Noll Plaza, Huntington, IN 46750; 1-800-348-2440

ISBN 978-1-61278-820-3 (Inventory No. T1626)
RELIGION / Spirituality; RELIGION / Christian Theology / Apologetics; RELIGION / Christianity / Catholic
eISBN: 978-1-61278-376-5
LCCN: 2015947024

Cover design: Lindsey Riesen
Cover art: *Christ Healing the Mother of Simon Peter's Wife*, by John Bridges (1818–1854); Private Collection Photo © Agnew's, London/Bridgeman Images.

PRINTED IN THE UNITED STATES OF AMERICA

CONTENTS

CHAPTER ONE

A Tsunami of the Spirit

*"Preach as you go, saying, 'The kingdom of heaven
is at hand.' Heal the sick, raise the dead,
cleanse lepers, cast out demons."*
— Matthew 10:7–8

*The kingdom of God does not consist
in talk but in power.*
— 1 Corinthians 4:20

It was a beautiful afternoon on the southern California coast, and 22-year-old Andrew Laubacher had just finished surfing. He was walking along the boardwalk in his wetsuit, heading back to his car, when he spotted a young girl sitting in a wheelchair on the beach. He knew he had to pray with her.

Andrew was in many ways a typical Catholic young adult. He loved surfing, playing music, and hanging out with his friends. In his teen years he had gone through a time of rebellion and had gotten into some trouble with the law. He had become an atheist for a time. Then he experienced a powerful conversion at a Steubenville Youth Conference,[1] and he began to learn that as followers of Christ we are called to bring the good news to others in the power of the Holy Spirit. He had even witnessed some miraculous healings. So when he saw the teenage Hispanic girl, sitting by the ocean in a wheelchair, he felt the prompting of the Holy Spirit to stop and pray with her. In his own words, Andrew recounts what happened next:

I got out of my wetsuit and dried off and approached the girl, who was with her parents. They didn't speak English but the girl did. I went up and asked how she was doing and if she wanted prayer for anything. The fear of rejection and of having nothing happen when I prayed was real and strong, but I went anyway.

As I asked her what was going on with her and why she was in a wheelchair, she began to pour out her life to me. It was shocking. She had just gotten out of the hospital because she had tried to kill herself for the second time. She had done meth and several other drugs, and she struggled with depression and anxiety. She had difficulty walking because she had had cerebral palsy since she was born. After she said all this, I was extremely moved with compassion and the conviction that God wanted to encounter her, and boldness came over me, casting out all fear that I was not good enough pray with her. So I prayed for healing for her condition, for peace and the power of the Holy Spirit to flood her body.

After I prayed for a little while I asked her to get up and walk. She began to walk and realized she was walking straighter and with less pain. Then I prayed over her knees. They visibly were crooked and sticking out in opposite directions, but after the prayer they were perfectly straight. When her parents saw that she was walking better and her knees were straightened out, they were shocked.

After all this I asked her what she was experiencing and she said her knees were hot and her body was tingling and there was no pain in her body. I told her, "That's Jesus, baby!" It

turned out she was Catholic but not into her faith
at all. I told her to get to Mass and confession
and receive the forgiveness that God wanted to
give her.

I stayed in touch with her after that day.
She texted me to tell me she went to confession
and Mass and said she felt free and lighter and
experienced the love of God.

After reflecting on that experience and
many more, I am convinced that, as the Scriptures say, the kingdom of God is not a matter of
talk but of power (1 Cor 4:20). As Christians, little "anointed ones," we can bring people healing
and redemption through Jesus everywhere we
go. We seem to do a lot of ministry and mission
trips, but what if every day in our very homes
we prayed with the sick, the depressed, the lame,
and the blind for healing? It would change everything. We would be manifesting the kingdom,
which is his love. This is our mission, to go out
into all the world and bring the good news of
healing, mercy, compassion, and most of all, unconditional love!

Because of Andrew's faith and courage in obeying the
prompting of the Holy Spirit, that young girl's life was changed
forever. If he had done nothing but talk to her about God's
love, that alone would have been a very good thing. However,
she might have thought to herself, "Sure, I know. I've heard all
that before." But because Andrew took the bold step of praying with her for healing, *she experienced God's love in her very
body.* In a most tangible way, this broken person encountered
the power and mercy of the risen Lord, restoring her to the
fullness of life.

I am convinced that Andrew's story represents something immensely significant that God is doing in the Church

in our time. The healing of the girl on the beach, while dramatic, is not unique. Thousands of similar healings have taken place around the world in recent years, as Catholics and other Christians have responded with new faith and fervor to the Lord's call to evangelize in the power of the Holy Spirit. In this age when so many have wandered far from God, the Lord is once more clothing his followers with power from on high (cf. Luke 24:49). He is calling us to go out and proclaim the gospel not only in words, but also in signs and wonders that bear witness to the truth of the words.

Healing is one of the charisms the Holy Spirit bestows on Christ's followers to equip us for mission. The gift of healing has been present in the Church in every age, but is being poured out in remarkable abundance in our time. Perhaps this is in part because of the tremendous physical, emotional, and spiritual woundedness in postmodern society. God has infinite compassion for those who suffer, and healing is one of the means he uses to manifest his real and powerful love.

There remain, however, many misconceptions about healing. Many Catholics assume miracles of healing are confined to the lives of great saints or to shrines like Lourdes, and that it is presumptuous for ordinary people to pray with expectation for such miracles. Many believe that God prefers his children to simply endure sickness or disability rather than to seek healing. Others would like to pray with people for healing, but are unsure how to go about it.

This book will seek to address these difficulties and answer questions like the following:

- Is Jesus really still healing people today?
- Are claimed miraculous healings authentic, and do they last?
- How do we know if God wants us to pray for healing?
- Who gets the gift of healing, and can I ask for it?
- How do I pray for healing?
- What if I pray and the person doesn't get healed?

- How does prayer for healing relate to the saints and sacraments?
- Does the Lord heal broken hearts as well as bodies?

The Tsunami of Secularism

To understand clearly what God is doing in relation to healing, we need to consider it within the broader context of our times. Christians in every age are called to read the signs of the times and interpret them in the light of the gospel.[2] We ought to regularly ask questions like these: What events and currents of thought are influencing the hearts and minds of people of our time? What are the global trends that will have an impact on future generations? What is the Lord calling us to do in response? What is the Spirit saying to the churches? (cf. Rev 2:7).

In October 2012, bishops from around the world were gathered in Rome for a synod on evangelization — three weeks of intense discussions on the current state of the Church and how to mobilize Catholics to spread the gospel. In an address to his fellow bishops, Cardinal Donald Wuerl of Washington, D.C., used a striking phrase: a "tsunami of secularism," he said, has engulfed the Western world.[3] With that phrase he captured the drama in which the Church is living today. The last few generations have witnessed an abandonment of Christian faith and a secularization of society on a scale never before seen in history. Vast numbers of people baptized as Christians are no longer practicing the faith and no longer have any connection with Christ or the Church. Many are living a practical Deism: they believe that perhaps in some sense God exists, but that he does not intervene in human history or act directly in our lives. The universe is a closed system in which everything can be explained by the laws of physics and biochemistry.

With the loss of Christian faith has come the denial of basic moral truths such as the inviolable dignity of human life and the sanctity of marriage. At the same time, a new kind of militant atheism has arisen, which not only argues against the existence of God, but ridicules Christianity and condemns all religions as equally irrational and dangerous. As Pope Benedict XVI wrote:

> In our days ... in vast areas of the world the faith is in danger of dying out like a flame which no longer has fuel.... The real problem at this moment of our history is that God is disappearing from the human horizon, and, with the dimming of the light which comes from God, humanity is losing its bearings, with increasingly evident destructive effects.[4]

The absence of God in our society leaves an inner void that people seek to fill with all kinds of counterfeits. There is a growing culture of narcissism, in which the highest values are ascribed to self-fulfillment, physical attractiveness, sexual freedom, and the accumulation of possessions. These empty pursuits have in turn led to a landscape of broken relationships, broken lives, loneliness, addiction, and the whole array of societal evils that St. John Paul II summed up as "the culture of death."[5]

A recent news item illustrates this profound darkness. A Belgian woman named Nancy Verhelst grew up with parents who treated her with utter contempt. "I was the girl that nobody wanted," she told a reporter. "While my brothers were celebrated, I got a storage room above the garage as a bedroom. 'If only you had been a boy,' my mother complained. I was tolerated, nothing more."[6] Perhaps it is not surprising that as an adult Nancy renamed herself Nathan and sought to remake herself as a man. We can only imagine the hurt and confusion of this broken person. But instead of offering her hope and healing, the best that a godless, secular society could do for her was provide sex-change surgery. After the operation, instead of feeling the peace she longed for, Nancy was disgusted with what she saw in the mirror and felt like a monster. And at that point, the best that a godless, secular society could do for her was to end her life. On September 30, 2013, Nancy was killed in an assisted suicide by lethal injection under Belgium's euthanasia law.

Truly, Satan is a tyrant — the thief who "comes only to steal and kill and destroy" (John 10:10). The world has become a war zone, where countless people are spiritually wounded and in dire need of help. A fierce battle is going on for the hearts and souls and minds of this generation. The stakes are high. What is going to meet the challenge of our times?

No human strategy or plan or program will suffice. It is God alone who holds the answer. "Not by might, nor by power, but by my Spirit, says the LORD of hosts" (Zech 4:6). The answer to the "tsunami of secularism" is nothing less than a *tsunami of the Spirit* — a proclamation of the gospel in the supernatural power of the Holy Spirit, accompanied by healings, signs, and wonders that tangibly demonstrate God's love and convince people that Jesus Christ is truly alive.

The Call to a New Evangelization

As society has descended into spiritual and moral darkness, the Church has been sounding a trumpet call to Christ's followers to let their light shine all the more brightly. For more than three decades the popes have been ringing out a summons to engage in a new evangelization — a renewed proclamation of the good news of Christ to the people of our time. The pontiffs have made clear that it is no longer only remote, unreached peoples who need to be evangelized but also, and especially, those in our own post-Christian society who no longer believe or practice the faith.

The summons actually began with Vatican Council II, when bishops and theologians were led to reflect deeply on the Church's evangelical mission. For centuries Catholics had been accustomed to thinking of evangelizing as a specialty work carried out only by priests or religious who are called to the foreign missions. The Council declared that in fact it is the duty of every Christian.[7] Following the Council, Blessed Pope Paul VI wrote an apostolic letter in which he affirmed, "Evangelizing is in fact the grace and vocation proper to the Church, her deepest identity. She exists in order to evangelize."[8]

John Paul II coined the term "New Evangelization," explaining that it is new not in content — it is the same gospel that has been preached for two millennia — but "in ardor, in method, and in expression."[9] It is new in *ardor* in that all Catholics need to be rekindled in a fire of zeal to proclaim Christ to others in both word and deed. It is new in *method* in that we must use methods adapted to our own time, including new and creative means of reaching people as well as up-to-date technologies. It is new in *expression* in that we cannot simply repeat formulas from the past but must speak in ways that touch the hearts and minds of this generation.

In 2001, John Paul II expressed the urgency of this task:

> Over the years, I have often repeated the summons to the *new evangelization.* I do so again now, especially in order to insist that we must rekindle in ourselves the impetus of the beginnings and allow ourselves to be filled with the ardor of the apostolic preaching which followed Pentecost. We must revive in ourselves the burning conviction of Paul, who cried out: "Woe to me if I do not preach the gospel!" (1 Cor 9:16).[10]

When Pope Benedict took office in 2005, he ensured that the New Evangelization would remain a long-term top priority for the Church, first by establishing a new Vatican department devoted to it, the Pontifical Council for Promoting the New Evangelization, and then by making it the theme of the 2012 World Synod of Bishops.

Pope Francis has given the call an even stronger urgency. In his apostolic letter *The Joy of the Gospel*, the follow-up document to the 2012 synod, he wrote:

> The new evangelization calls for personal involvement on the part of each of the baptized. Every Christian is challenged, here and now, to be actively engaged in evangelization; indeed, anyone who has truly experienced God's saving love does not need much time or lengthy training to go out and proclaim that love. Every Christian is a missionary to the extent that he or she has encountered the love of God in Christ Jesus: we no longer say that we are "disciples" and "missionaries," but rather that we are always "missionary disciples."[11]

Pope Francis insists that the call to evangelization demands a complete retooling and re-visioning of the way parishes and other church institutions function. All are to become completely mission-oriented. "In all its activities the parish encourages and trains its members to be evangelizers."[12] From now on "we 'cannot passively and calmly wait in our church buildings'; we need to move 'from a pastoral ministry of mere conservation to a decidedly missionary pastoral ministry.'"[13]

It would be hard to imagine stronger exhortations from the Church's pastors. Yet it must be admitted that the New Evangelization has yet to take hold in a truly radical way. While many parishes and dioceses have made diligent efforts in responding to the call, often these efforts have resulted in relatively meager fruit. In some areas, the faithful do not yet know what the "New Evangelization" is. In others, it has become simply the latest catchphrase. Evangelization is sometimes interpreted to mean simply "everything we're already doing," and New Evangelization means simply "more of the same." In many areas of the western world, the number of practicing Catholics continues in rapid decline.

Clearly, something is missing; something more is needed to awaken the Catholic Church. What will light a fire of evangelistic fervor in the hearts and minds of Catholics of the twenty-first century and enable them to proclaim the good news in a convincing way to the people of our time?

The First Evangelization

This question can only be answered adequately by taking a closer look at the *first* evangelization — the explosion of Christianity in the ancient world — and learning how it was that a tiny, ragtag band of Christians "turned the world upside down" for Christ (as was literally said of Christians in Acts 17:6). How did this little community of former fishermen, tax collectors, prostitutes, slaves, and ordinary people, while being subjected to waves of violent state persecution, so convince the world of the gospel that by the time Christianity finally became legal, and thus safe, in the early fourth century, Christians were already nearly a quarter of the population of the Roman Empire?[14]

The beginnings of this first evangelization are recounted in the New Testament, especially in the Gospels and Acts. These books give us the divinely inspired account of what the Church's mission is meant to look like. The New Testament is not only a source of doctrine or of interesting historical data about early Christianity, but also the blueprint for the life and mission of the Church today. The apostolic Church contains the DNA, so to speak, for the Church in every age. Awakening Catholics to their evangelistic mission today therefore means taking a closer look at what Scripture itself reveals about that first evangelization.

Another reason the apostolic Church merits closer attention is that today we find ourselves in a cultural situation that is in some respects more like that faced by the early Christians than it has been at any time since. There is growing hostility to Christianity and intense social pressure to keep our faith to ourselves and stay out of the public square. Vast numbers of people are living an essentially pagan, hedonistic lifestyle. Many are completely ignorant of the gospel. This fact was vividly brought home to a religious sister I know who walked into a drugstore one day wearing her crucifix. Seeing it, the girl behind the counter innocently asked, "Oh, who's the man hanging on that bar? My grandmother had one of those."

In some ways we face an even more challenging situation than the early Christians did. Many people today have been exposed to just enough Christianity to be inoculated against it. They think they know essentially everything there is to know about Jesus and the Church. They have been influenced by a constant media barrage of references to Christian violence, colonialism, hypocrisy, hostility to science, and sexual crimes — some accurate, and many exaggerated or false. They rarely hear anything about the vast amount of good Christians do. People formed in these circumstances are far more difficult to reach than those who have never heard of Jesus.

In the biblical account of the first evangelization, one factor that is immediately obvious is the prominent role played by healings and other miraculous works of God. For Jesus and his first followers, the preaching of the good news was inseparable from the signs and wonders by which God himself corroborated the spoken message and convinced the hearers of its truth. As the letter to the Hebrews puts it, while Christians preached the word, "God also bore witness by signs and wonders and various miracles and by gifts of the Holy Spirit distributed according to his own will" (Heb 2:4). Through these miracles done through faith in the name of Jesus, countless people personally witnessed Christ's power and came to believe in him.

Are people today any less in need of an encounter with God than the people of the first century? In a world that has lost a sense of the transcendent, healings and miracles are all the more needed to demonstrate that God is the living God who acts in history and in human lives. They are a balm for the gaping spiritual wound in contemporary society: the wound of the absence of God. Healings convince even the most hardened and broken hearts that God has not left us orphans but is present and active and rich in mercy toward us. At the same time, they remind believers that evangelization relies less on human resources than on the Holy Spirit, the principal agent of evangelization.[15] Healings are part of God's providential answer to the spiritual darkness of our times.

Prayer for Healing

Most Catholics are used to praying for the sick. We do so at the liturgy, at special events, and in private whenever we hear of someone who is ill or injured.

But it is something else to pray *with* and *over* a sick person, confidently asking the Lord to heal him or her. That is outside the box for many Catholics. Many are not sure whether it is even legitimate to do so. Isn't it prideful to expect God to work a healing at *my* request? I'm not worthy to be used like that. I don't pray enough. I'm not virtuous enough. I fail too often. I can barely get through the day, much less live up to the holiness of the saints.

This hesitation is understandable, but it is based on a serious misconception. The truth is that God pours out his gifts, including the gift of healing, freely. He desires to give this gift far more abundantly than we think. He is not limited by our abilities, but only by our faith and our desire to be used by him. "By the power at work within us [he] is able to do far more abundantly than all that we ask or think" (Eph 3:20).

As someone who grew up Catholic, I too have prayed for the sick all my life. For nearly thirty years I have also often prayed *with* people for healing, sometimes with the laying on of hands. Only rarely did I witness even a slight improvement — a stomach feeling better or a headache gradually disappearing. But in the last three years, after observing and learning from those who have great faith for healing, especially Randy Clark and Damian Stayne,[16] I have begun to see people healed on a regular basis, sometimes in amazing ways. The difference is that I pray now with greater faith that the Lord really does want to heal, and loves to heal, his children who are broken and hurting. I also offer to pray with people much more often than before. I have become convinced that miraculous healing is not meant to be something rare but ordinary in the life of the Church, and that the Lord does not want to use only spiritual superstars with special gifts, but every "little ole' me," as Randy Clark puts it.

In this book I share what I have learned from studying what Scripture, theology, and Church history have to tell us about healing, as well as my own experience and that of friends and co-laborers in the Lord's vineyard. My hope is that you too will gain confidence to pray with others with expectant faith for healing, even in the most unexpected times and places, as Andrew did on the beach. As we pursue the daunting task of evangelizing the people of the twenty-first century, the Church needs the full endowment of supernatural gifts given to her by her living Lord. The Lord longs to lavish these gifts on his children so they in turn can lavish his mercy on the world. Obtaining these gifts is not complicated, but simple. "Ask, and it will be given you" (Matt 7:7).

CHAPTER TWO

The Kingdom Is at Hand

Surely he has borne our infirmities
and carried our diseases;
yet we accounted him stricken,
struck down by God, and afflicted.
But he was wounded for our transgressions,
crushed for our iniquities;
upon him was the punishment that made us whole,
and by his bruises we are healed.

— *Isaiah 53:4–5*

In the ancient world, leprosy was a deadly and terrifying disease. Besides the disfiguring sores, the oozing pus, and the shame of being considered accursed by God, lepers were social outcasts. They were required by the law of Moses to live apart from human society, and wherever they went they had to rend their garments and shout, "Unclean, unclean" (Lev 13:45). Because their condition caused ritual impurity, they were even barred from participating in the high point of Jewish life: the worship of God in his holy temple in Jerusalem.

As Jesus was traveling from village to village in Galilee, a leper approached him with surprising boldness. This man must have heard the rumors about Jesus, the prophet from Nazareth who was healing the sick, and in his desperation he resolved to act. Braving the disapproval and disgust of others, he came and knelt before Jesus and voiced his plea: "If you will, you can make me clean" (Mark 1:40).

Seeing the man's wretched condition, Jesus was "moved with compassion." The Greek word means physically churned up or stirred with gut-wrenching emotion. It was the deeply human reaction of the Son of God. Jesus never looked upon afflicted people with detachment or indifference, but always with the empathy that comes from knowing the human condition from within. We can imagine the love in his eyes as he replied, "I *do* will it. Be made clean." Does he will to make a man whole, to undo the ravages of the fall? This is what he came for!

According to the law of Moses, any contact with a leper would render a person unclean. The crowd standing nearby must have gasped in astonishment as they watched Jesus deliberately reach out and touch the man. And before their eyes, the leprosy disappeared. The Old Testament rules of ritual purity had been turned on their head! Instead of the unclean contaminating the clean, the clean had triumphed, as was indisputably proven by the fact that the man was no longer a leper. Jesus' holiness is invincible. No defilement can contaminate him; rather, he removes defilement from whoever approaches him in faith. It is a powerful message for those who feel unworthy even to approach him.

Jesus instructed the healed man to keep quiet about his healing, to show himself to a priest, and to offer the sacrifice prescribed in the law of Moses for the cleansing of skin disease. The prescribed rite was to take two birds, one to be sacrificed and the other, dipped in the blood of the first, to fly away free (Lev 14:3–7). If the man obeyed these instructions, before his eyes was a vivid symbolic image of what Jesus had just done for him. One is sacrificed; another is set free. Although he could not have understood it then, this man had been set free from leprosy at the cost of Christ's own blood, soon to be shed on the cross.

Unable to contain his joy, the newly healed man began to spread far and wide the news of what Jesus had done for him — that is, he began to evangelize. The Greek text literally says "he began to talk freely about it, and to spread the news" (Mark 1:45), wording that is clearly suggestive of the Christian proclamation of the gospel after Pentecost.

As a result of this undesired publicity, Jesus was now so mobbed by crowds that he could no longer enter a village. Ironically, the Lord had traded places with the leper. The once-outcast man was now free to enter society, and Jesus had become the outcast. This reversal is another sign of the fact that all Jesus' healings took place at a cost to himself — ultimately, the cost of his own life. The healing of the leper foreshadows the cross, the source from which all Christ's works of healing flow.

This healing is thus a kind of real-life parable, an image of what Christ has done for us. Who is the leper? I am. We all are. All have been deformed and debilitated by the devastating consequences of sin — spiritually, emotionally, and often physically. We all experience to some degree the inner shame that comes from sin, the alienation from God and others that it causes. God was moved with such compassion for us that he sent his only Son to become man, to take upon himself sin and all its consequences and bear them in his own body on the cross.

Often people in need of healing are troubled by an underlying doubt: "I'm not worthy to be healed." But whoever has that thought can settle it easily. It is in fact true: in ourselves we are not worthy. "Lord, I am not worthy to have you come under my roof," as the centurion said to Jesus (Matt 8:8), and we say before receiving him in the Eucharist. But Jesus has *made us worthy* by shedding his blood for us. As the letter to the Hebrews says, "we have confidence ... by the blood of Jesus"; "Let us then with confidence draw near to the throne of grace, that we may receive mercy and find grace to help in time of need" (Heb 10:19; 4:16). As the leper's confidence in approaching Jesus was richly rewarded, so will ours be. Jesus wants to take our place — to take away our sickness, our shame, our sin — and restore us to the fullness of life. He will even be the outcast if need be.

Anointed by the Spirit to Heal

The cleansing of the leper, near the beginning of Jesus' public ministry, presaged the prominent role healings would play in his mission. Many people tend to think of healings as second-ary to Jesus' real purpose, to save souls. But the Gospels tell us otherwise. In the biblical understanding, the human person is an inseparable unity of body and soul. Christ came not just to "save souls" but to *save human beings* — to raise us up, body and soul, to the fullness of divine life in communion with God and all the redeemed forever. The body therefore has inestimable significance in God's plan. It will one day be radiant with divine life (1 Cor 15:42–49). Jesus' healings of bodily sickness and infirmity are a foreshadowing of the glo-rious destiny of the human body.

Twenty-one percent of the Gospel accounts of Jesus' public ministry is devoted to reports of his physical healings and exorcisms — a striking percentage when one considers the length and importance of his teachings, not to mention other miracles such as the multiplication of loaves and the calming of the storm. Clearly, Jesus' healings are not a minor element or peripheral to his real purpose.

When the Synoptic Gospels (Matthew, Mark, and Luke) summarize Jesus' activity during his public ministry, they invariably mention healings.

> He went about all Galilee, teaching in their syna-gogues and preaching the gospel of the kingdom and healing every disease and every infirmity among the people. (Matt 4:23)

> He healed many who were sick with various dis-eases, and cast out many demons. (Mark 1:34)

A great multitude of people from all Judea and
Jerusalem and the seacoast of Tyre and Sidon …
came to hear him and to be healed of their diseases; and those who were troubled with unclean
spirits were cured. And all the crowd sought to
touch him, for power came forth from him and
healed them all. (Luke 6:17–19)

Why such an emphasis on healing? The explanation is
provided by Jesus himself in his first sermon, delivered in his
hometown of Nazareth soon after his baptism (Luke 4:16–
21). The Gospel of Luke highlights this sermon as providing
the interpretive key to Jesus' whole mission:

He came to Nazareth, where he had been
brought up; and he went to the synagogue, as
was his custom, on the sabbath day. And he
stood up to read; and there was given to him
the book of the prophet Isaiah. He opened the
book and found the place where it was written,

"The Spirit of the Lord is upon me,
because he has anointed me to preach good
news to the poor.
He has sent me to proclaim release to the
captives
and recovering of sight to the blind,
to set at liberty those who are oppressed,
to proclaim the acceptable year of the Lord."

And he closed the book, and gave it back to the
attendant, and sat down; and the eyes of all in
the synagogue were fixed on him. And he began
to say to them, "Today this Scripture has been
fulfilled in your hearing."

The sense of anticipation in this scene is palpable. The
synagogue attendees seem aware that Jesus is about to say

something of immense significance, and indeed he does. Having read from Isaiah 61, a passage that foretells the Messiah, the long-promised and long-awaited deliverer of Israel, Jesus announces that the promise is fulfilled in him.[17]

Jesus chose precisely *this* passage to define the essence of his mission. "The Spirit of the Lord is upon me" refers to his baptism in the Jordan River, described just a few verses earlier, when the Holy Spirit descended on him in the form of a dove (Luke 3:22). "He has anointed me" means that on that occasion God the Father filled him with the Holy Spirit, empowering him for his mission as Messiah. His very title, Messiah (or in Greek, Christ), means "Anointed One" and derives from that anointing at his baptism.[18] As Tertullian, a third-century Church Father, explains, "He is called Christ because he was anointed by the Father with the Holy Spirit."[19] Although Jesus was filled with the Holy Spirit from the moment of his conception, it was with the anointing at his baptism that his human nature was fully endowed with divine power for his messianic mission.

The Isaiah passage also describes the mission itself. The purpose of Jesus' anointing was so that he could "proclaim good news to the poor" — good news that includes not only hopeful words but the *very realities* that the words announce: freedom, healing, and release from captivity. The "poor" are both the materially poor and all people, spiritually impoverished by their alienation from God. By applying this Scripture text to himself, Jesus is declaring that he has been anointed by the Holy Spirit in order to go into places of deep human bondage, of blindness, sickness, and oppression, to proclaim the good news of the kingdom and visibly manifest it by setting people free. Healing and deliverance are not peripheral but at the very heart of his mission.

In Acts, when the apostle Peter gives a brief summary of Jesus' public ministry, he too puts healing and deliverance at its center. Peter tells the crowd gathered in the house of

Cornelius, "God anointed Jesus of Nazareth with the Holy Spirit and with power ... he went about doing good and healing all that were oppressed by the devil, for God was with him" (Acts 10:38).

The Lord Your Healer

In response to a complaint from the Pharisees, Jesus gave a further insight into his mission. When he sat at table with tax collectors and sinners, people normally excluded from the company of the pious, the Pharisees were scandalized. Jesus replied to their objections with a kind of proverb: "Those who are well have no need of a physician, but those who are sick" (Luke 5:31). He thereby identified himself as a physician, and his mission as one of healing.

As Jesus' hearers probably understood, he was hinting at his divine identity, for Scripture speaks of *God* as the healer of his people. In Exodus, after leading his people out of slavery and across the Red Sea, God had revealed something new about himself. He gave himself a new name: "I am the LORD, your healer" (Exod 15:26). With this title God indicates that healing springs from his very nature. It belongs to his very character to restore his people to wholeness, because he desires the fullness of life for them.

Jesus' healings, then, reveal him as the divine Healer present in the midst of his people. His whole mission can be described as a work of healing, a restoration of souls and bodies to the fullness of life that God intended. The word "health," in fact, comes from the same root as "whole" and "holy." Healing in the fullest sense is becoming whole in spirit, soul, and body. And because God created us for himself, wholeness is nothing other than holiness — a union of love with the all-holy God.

Saving and Healing

In response to another complaint about his fraternizing with sinners — in this case, Zacchaeus the tax collector — Jesus summed up his mission with a succinct phrase: "the Son of Man came to seek and to save the lost" (Luke 19:10). The Greek verb for "save" (*sōzō*) can also be translated "heal"; it is the same word used in many of his healings.[20] The Gospels do not allow us to create an artificial separation between Jesus' healing of bodies and his saving of souls, as if only the second really counts; rather, they are two dimensions of his one work of healing-salvation.

As Pope Benedict XVI wrote in his book *Jesus of Nazareth*, "Healing is an essential dimension of the apostolic mission and of Christian faith in general." It can even be said that Christianity is a "'therapeutic religion' — a religion of healing…. When understood at a sufficiently deep level, this expresses the entire content of 'redemption.'"[21] Jesus ultimately came to heal humanity's deepest wound: the wound of our sin and consequent alienation from God, with all its consequences of spiritual and physical brokenness.

Jesus once again placed healing at the heart of his messianic mission when John the Baptist sent messengers to inquire whether he was truly the Messiah foretold by the prophets. John had been chained up in prison by Herod — a part of God's plan that he had probably not foreseen at all — and he was tempted to doubt and discouragement. Jesus pointed to his healings as the clue to the answer.

> They said, "John the Baptist has sent us to you, saying, 'Are you he who is to come, or shall we look for another?'" In that hour he cured many of diseases and plagues and evil spirits, and on many that were blind he bestowed sight. And he answered them, "Go and tell John what you have seen and heard: the blind receive their sight, the

lame walk, lepers are cleansed, and the deaf hear,
the dead are raised up, the poor have good news
preached to them." (Luke 7:20–22)

With this reply Jesus recalls the biblical passages that
foretold the messianic age as a time of abundant healings. Isaiah had prophesied:

"Then the eyes of the blind shall be opened,
  and the ears of the deaf unstopped;
then shall the lame man leap like a dear,
  and the tongue of the mute sing for joy." (Isa 35:5–6;
  see Isa 29:18; 42:7)

Before the eyes of John's messengers, Jesus proceeded to
fulfill these very promises by restoring sight to the blind and
curing others of disease and demonic oppression. He is indeed
"the one who is to come."

Signs of the Kingdom

Jesus' healings are inseparable from his preaching of the kingdom of God. He began his public ministry by announcing the
arrival of the kingdom (Mark 1:15); then he demonstrated it
by his healings and miracles. In Jesus' very presence, in his
words and deeds, the reign of God has been inaugurated on
earth. The dominion of Satan has been broken and the restoration of all creation has begun.

As Jesus says in the Gospel of John, "the works which
the Father has given me to accomplish, these very works which
I am doing, bear me witness that the Father has sent me" (John
5:36).[22] This saying does not mean that his works are merely
external proofs of his divinity, as if he did them simply to convince people that he is who he says he is. In fact, more often
than not his miracles turned the religious authorities against
him.[23] Rather, the miracles are the *embodiment* of the good

news itself: that he is the long-awaited Messiah who has come to overthrow every kind of evil and restore God's people to the fullness of life.

To convey this deeper understanding of Jesus' works, the Gospel of John prefers to call them *signs* rather than miracles. Each of the miracles, perceived with the eyes of faith, *signifies* something. Each reveals an aspect of Jesus' identity and mission. His turning of water into wine at Cana reveals that he is the bridegroom of the messianic wedding (John 2:1–11; 3:25). His multiplication of loaves reveals that he is the bread of life (John 6:35). His healing of the blind man reveals that he is the light of the world, who brings us out of spiritual darkness (John 9:5). His raising of Lazarus reveals that he is the resurrection and the life (John 11:25). Jesus heals and gives life because it is his very nature, as God, to do so. All his works are meant to lead us into the mystery of his divine identity and messianic mission.

Scripture often uses the phrase "signs and wonders" to speak of the miracles God did through Moses during the exodus.[24] In Acts 2:22 Peter uses these same words for Jesus' miracles to show that Jesus has accomplished the new and greater exodus — the redemption of his people from slavery to sin. Jesus' healings are *signs* because they signify his definitive victory over sin and all its consequences, his inauguration of the kingdom, and the beginning of the "last days" (Acts 2:17). They are *wonders* because they provoke wonder, awe, praise, and gratitude in those who witness them.[25]

He Healed Them All

Reading the Gospels one gets the strong impression that Jesus was not only willing but eager to heal. The Gospels repeatedly affirm the unlimited scope of his healings.

> They brought him *all the sick*, those afflicted with various diseases and pains, demoniacs, epileptics, and paralytics, and he healed them. (Matt 4:24)

> [He] healed *all who were sick.* (Matt 8:16; cf. Mark 1:32)

> Jesus went about all the cities and villages, teaching in their synagogues and preaching the gospel of the kingdom, and healing *every disease and every infirmity.* (Matt 9:35)

> They sent round to all that region and brought to him *all that were sick,* and begged him that they might only touch the fringe of his garment; and as many as touched it were made well. (Matt 14:35–36; cf. Mark 8:56)

> *All* those who had any that were sick with various diseases brought them to him; and he laid his hands on *every one of them* and healed them. (Luke 4:40)

> All the crowd sought to touch him, for power came forth from him and healed them *all.* (Luke 6:19)

Everywhere Jesus went he was besieged by the sick and infirm. Nowhere do the Gospels record that he instructed a person simply to bear the suffering assigned to them. In no case does he indicate that a person is asking for too much and should be content with a partial healing or no healing. He invariably treats illness as an evil to be overcome rather than a good to be embraced.[26]

Jesus does not always respond immediately to the demands of the needy crowds. On a few occasions, he withdraws to be alone with the Father in prayer and then to move on to his next destination (Mark 1:35–38; Luke 5:15–16). It is also reasonable to infer that Jesus did not heal every sick person within reach. At the pool of Bethesda, there lay "a multitude of invalids, blind, lame, paralyzed" (John 5:3), but the Gospel mentions his speaking to and curing only one lame man. In Acts, Peter and John heal a crippled man who was a well-known beggar at the temple gate (Acts 3:1–10); presumably Jesus had passed by him many times at this gate and had not healed him. He left something for his apostles to do! There are also instances in which Jesus initially seems to refuse a request, but then in response to persistent faith does perform a miracle (the Canaanite woman in Matthew 15:20–28, the official with a sick son in John 4:46–53, and Mary at Cana in John 2:1–11).[27] However, the Gospels record no instance in which a person asks Jesus for healing and is categorically refused.

This evidence from Scripture ought to challenge our accustomed ideas about the Lord's will to heal. Have we too easily accepted the idea that sickness should simply be embraced? Do we too easily assume that if a person is ill, God wants her to remain that way for her good? Could our resignation to illness or infirmity even sometimes be a cloak for unbelief? Scripture does not say that the Lord will always heal in response to our prayer if only we have enough faith. Jesus instructs his followers not only to heal the sick but also to "visit" them (Matt 25:36), and Paul's letters refer to cases where sickness remains, at least for a time, despite his own charism of healing (Gal 4:13; Phil 2:26–27; 1 Tim 5:23; 2 Tim 4:20). However, it *is* reasonable to conclude that the Lord desires to heal far more often than we think.

Healing on the Sabbath

It is well known that Jesus often healed on the Sabbath, provoking the fury of scribes and Pharisees who regarded healings as work, which was prohibited on the Sabbath (Luke 13:14; John 5:16). A less well-known but striking fact is that *every healing that Jesus himself initiated* was on the Sabbath. Jesus responded to requests from sick people, or their parents or friends, on any day of the week. But wherever the Gospels record healings he did apart from any request, they are on the Sabbath. On the Sabbath Jesus restored a man's withered hand, straightened the back of a woman who had been bent over for eighteen years, cured a man with dropsy (water retention), made a crippled man walk, gave sight to a man born blind, and delivered a demon-possessed man.[28]

This pattern is no mere coincidence. Jesus' evident preference for healing on the Sabbath is, like the healings themselves, a sign giving insight into who he is. In response to the Jewish leaders who complained that he was breaking the Sabbath, he revealed something else about his identity: "the Son of man is Lord even of the sabbath" (Mark 2:28). This claim does not mean only that he has authority to interpret the Sabbath laws, to decide what does or does not count as work. Rather, Jesus is revealing that he is the Lord who instituted the Sabbath in the first place and who fulfills its deepest meaning.

The book of Genesis records God's establishment of the Sabbath as a day of rest (Gen 2:2-3), the day when human beings cease from work to enjoy their unique privilege of relating to God. It is also the day when God's people remember that they were once slaves in Egypt, but the Lord set them free (Deut 5:15). The Sabbath is therefore far more than a time to rest up so as to get back to work with renewed energy. The Sabbath is a sign of our highest dignity — our covenant relationship with God — and of the freedom and joy that come from communion with him. The fact that Jesus chose to heal especially on the Sabbath signifies that he is "lord of the sabbath" (Matt 12:8; Luke 6:5) in the sense that he has come to inaugurate the *new* creation by which human beings are restored to the fullness of life that God intended from the beginning.

Jesus' inaugural sermon in the synagogue at Nazareth, quoted earlier (on page 27), reveals the same truth in a different way. The last line of the passage from Isaiah says the Messiah would proclaim "the acceptable year of the Lord," or in other translations (such as the New International Version), "the year of the Lord's favor." As the audience would have well understood, Isaiah was referring to the jubilee year, one of the sacred celebrations decreed by God in the law of Moses (Lev 25). The jubilee was to be held every fiftieth year. During the jubilee, all debts were canceled, all slaves were set free, and all ancestral lands that had been sold off due to debt or impoverishment were returned to their original owner. The jubilee was a time of freedom, joy, and celebration. Isaiah was prophesying that the coming of the Messiah would be the ultimate jubilee — a jubilee that would never end. By saying "This passage has been fulfilled in your hearing," Jesus proclaims that in him, that never-ending jubilee of the Lord has arrived.

The Gospels thus invite us to understand Jesus' healings in light of God's original intention for human beings, created in his image and likeness. Sickness and disability were not part of God's plan for creation but are outward symptoms of the damage caused by the Fall. God designed human beings with bodies meant to radiate the splendor of divine life present within them. He endowed us with not only the physical senses but also marvelous spiritual capacities to see, hear, and relate to him. Original sin caused our bodies to become corruptible and our interior faculties to be disabled, resulting in a communication block between God and humanity. Jesus' healings of people who were deaf, blind, lame, and paralyzed are a sign of his restoration of humanity to wholeness and unbroken communion with our Creator. Although that restoration will only be complete at the resurrection of the dead (1 Cor 15:42–53), already by the grace of Christ we are able to hear God's voice in our hearts, see him with the eyes of faith, walk in friendship with him, sing his praises, and proclaim his mighty deeds.

As St. Irenaeus wrote, "The glory of God is man fully alive."[29]

The Cost of Healings

As the story of the leper suggests, Jesus' works of healing and deliverance came at a cost. Although he healed people for free, those healings were at the cost *to himself* of his own bodily sacrifice. The Gospel of Matthew explains that this cost was all part of God's plan, revealed in Scripture:

> That evening they brought to him many who were possessed with demons; and he cast out the spirits with a word, and healed all who were sick. This was to fulfill what was spoken by the prophet Isaiah, "He took our infirmities and bore our diseases." (Matt 8:16–17)[30]

Matthew is quoting from Isaiah 53, the fourth song of the suffering Servant of the Lord. Early Christian tradition recognized this passage as the most explicit prophecy of Christ's passion to be found in the Old Testament.[31] The song speaks of the Servant bearing not only the *sins* of God's people (vv. 5–6, 10, 12), but also their infirmities and diseases (v. 4).[32] Matthew sees this mention of infirmities and diseases as pointing in a special way to Christ's healings of the sick and demon-possessed.[33] The Hebrew meaning of the verbs "took" and "bore" is significant. They refer to the Servant not only *removing* afflictions but *taking them on* himself. Matthew is, of course, not saying that Jesus became sick or demon-possessed, but that in a mysterious way he bore these afflictions, along with our sins, in his own body on the cross. His power to heal flows from his own vicarious suffering of sin and all its consequences.

Jesus' healings foreshadow not only his passion; they also point to his resurrection from the dead. The Gospels hint at this link every time they use the word "raised up" or "rose" for those healed by Jesus. When Jesus cured Peter's mother-in-law of a fever, he took her by the hand and "raised her up" (Mark 1:31). He commanded the paralytic, "Rise, take up your pallet and go home," and the man "rose" (Mark 2:11–12). He said to Jairus' dead daughter, "Little girl, I say to you, arise!" and she "got up and walked" (Mark 5:41–42). He took the epileptic boy by the hand, "raised him up," and the boy "arose" (Mark 9:27). In each case, these are the same verbs used for Jesus' resurrection (Mark 16:6, 9, 14; 16:9), and for the resurrection of all the dead on the last day.[34]

Jesus' healings of physical afflictions, while marvelous for those who receive them, are only a pale shadow of the ultimate healing he will accomplish in the end, when our bodies are transformed to be like his glorified body and the new creation is fully revealed. As St. Paul wrote, "When the perishable puts on the imperishable, and the mortal puts on immortality, then shall come to pass the saying that is written: 'Death is swallowed up in victory'" (1 Cor 15:54). "For this slight momentary affliction is preparing for us an eternal weight of glory beyond all comparison" (2 Cor 4:17; cf. Rom 8:18–19).

Jesus' Commission to His Followers

Everywhere Jesus went, teaching, healing, and casting out demons, people saw the promises of God being fulfilled before their eyes. The kingdom of God was being manifested in their midst. The Gospels give not the slightest warrant for the idea that these signs of the arrival of the kingdom were to cease after Jesus' ascension into heaven. Rather, Jesus commissioned his followers to continue his saving mission by doing just as he had done.

During his public ministry, Jesus sent out the twelve apostles on a kind of practice mission. He commanded them, "Preach as you go, saying, 'The kingdom of heaven is at hand.' Heal the sick, raise the dead, cleanse lepers, cast out demons" (Matt 10:7-8). They were not to preach the kingdom in word alone, but to demonstrate it with deeds of power. They could accomplish these mighty works not by any ability of their own but by the authority he delegated to them (10:1). Luke records that Jesus later commissioned a larger group of seventy. He gave them the same charge: "Whenever you enter a town and they receive you … heal the sick in it and say to them, 'The kingdom of God has come near to you'" (Luke 10:8-10).

During Jesus' earthly life the commission was only for these chosen delegates. But after his resurrection, the risen Lord extended the authority to heal and cast out demons to all believers. Among the signs that would accompany "those who believe," i.e., Christians, he said, "in my name they will cast out demons;… they will lay their hands on the sick, and they will recover" (Mark 16:17-18).[35] He also affirmed that "they will speak in new tongues; they will pick up serpents, and if they drink any deadly thing, it will not hurt them" — that is, they will experience divine protection from evil. Now all believers, filled with the Spirit of the risen Lord, are gifted with supernatural power for their mission to "preach good news to the poor" (Luke 4:18).

The early Christians took Jesus' words at face value. And the Lord vindicated their faith by doing abundant miracles through them, as the next chapter will describe.

CHAPTER THREE

Healing in the Age of
the Apostles

*Now many signs and wonders were done among
the people by the hands of the apostles....
And more than ever believers were added to the Lord,
multitudes of both men and women.*

— Acts 5:12–14

Before his ascension to heaven, Jesus gave his apostles a solemn commission to continue his work on earth. They must have been eager to embark on this mission. However, there was one important thing that had to occur before they could begin. Jesus instructed them, "Stay in the city until you are clothed with power from on high" (Luke 24:49). The same charge is repeated in Acts: "He ordered them not to depart from Jerusalem, but to wait for the promise of the Father," namely, that they would be "baptized with the Holy Spirit" (Acts 1:4–5). Only by being filled with the Holy Spirit, as Jesus was at his own baptism, would they have the divine power they needed to be his witnesses to all nations.

Luke records that after giving this instruction, Jesus "was lifted up, and a cloud took him out of their sight. And while they were gazing into heaven as he went, behold, two men stood by them in white robes ..." (Acts 1:9–10). A cloud had great significance for the people of Israel. In the time of the exodus, the cloud was the visible sign of God's presence in the midst of his people (Exod 40:34–38). Moses had gone up

Mount Sinai, enveloped in a cloud, and brought down the gift of the Torah. So now Jesus goes up to heaven in a cloud and will bring down an infinitely greater gift, the Holy Spirit (Exod 19:9; Acts 2:33).

The two men in white robes are also a clue to what is happening. When was Jesus last seen in a cloud? At his transfiguration. The two men with him then were Moses and Elijah (Luke 9:28–35).

Moses, the great leader of Israel, had a young assistant named Joshua who spent years at his side, being formed by him and watching him do miracles as he led Israel out of slavery into freedom. Before Moses died he imparted his spirit to Joshua to succeed him in leadership (Deut 34:9). Joshua went on to do what he had seen Moses do: he led the Israelites across water on dry ground (Josh 3), a replay of the crossing of the Red Sea, and went on to lead them to victory in battle against their enemies.

Elijah too had a disciple, Elisha, who spent years with him, being formed by him and watching him prophesy, do signs and wonders, and call Israel to conversion. On the day Elijah was about to be taken up to heaven, he said to Elisha, "Ask what I shall do for you, before I am taken from you" (2 Kgs 2:9). Elisha's response was bold: he begged for a "double portion" of Elijah's spirit, i.e., his supernatural gifting for prophecy, signs and wonders. In biblical tradition, a firstborn son received a double portion of the inheritance. Elisha was in effect asking to be Elijah's firstborn, to be just like him. Elijah answered, "You have asked something that is not easy. Still, if you see me taken up from you, your wish will be granted; otherwise not." As he was taken up in a flaming chariot, Elisha did indeed see him — the sign that his desire was granted. And he immediately did just what he had seen his master do: striking the water of the Jordan with Elijah's mantle, he crossed over on dry ground (2 Kgs 2:14). He went on to perform many healings and miracles, calling Israel to conversion just as Elijah had done.

This biblical background helps us understand the gift that Jesus imparts to his apostles and to the whole Church. As he ascends into heaven, they *see* him — the sign that they will indeed receive a "double portion" of his Holy Spirit, empowering them to continue his mission. That promise is fulfilled at Pentecost, when the Holy Spirit falls on the hundred and twenty disciples gathered in the upper room, with the rush of a mighty wind and "tongues as of fire" (Acts 2:1–4). Like Joshua and Elisha, Jesus' followers then go on to do just what they had seen their Master do: proclaim the good news with signs and wonders in the power of the Holy Spirit.

The Lame Man at the Beautiful Gate

The first event after the outpouring of the Holy Spirit at Pentecost, as Luke reports it, is the healing of the lame man at the Beautiful Gate of the temple (Acts 3). It is a dramatic demonstration of the power of the risen Jesus now at work in his disciples.

Peter and John were on their way into the temple at three o'clock, the traditional hour of the evening sacrifice. Few knew it was an hour now made sacred by Christ's death on the cross (Luke 23:44). The scene was probably similar to that of a city church today at the time just before Sunday Mass — a stream of worshipers moving toward the doors, a panhandler or two on the steps, noise, bustle, and distraction. The crippled man hardly glanced at Peter and John among the jostling crowd as he begged for a handout.

But Peter, newly filled with the Holy Spirit, must have been prompted by the Spirit to know that this was to be no ordinary encounter. He "gazed intently" at the man and said to him, "Look at us," and the man "fixed his attention on them" (3:4–5). What was important about this intense look? On a natural level, it engaged the man's full attention, establishing a relationship between him and the two apostles.

But Luke hints at more. The Greek verb for "gaze intently" is *atenizō*. It means "to keep one's eyes fixed on," and is used in Acts especially in supernatural contexts: the apostles gazing into heaven at Jesus' ascension (1:10); the Jewish leaders gazing at Stephen as his face became like that of an angel (6:15); Stephen gazing into heaven (7:55); Cornelius gazing at an angel (10:4); Peter gazing at a heavenly vision (11:6). Strikingly, the word appears in a miracle story that closely parallels this one: Paul's healing of a lame man at Lystra. "Paul, gazing intently at him and seeing that he had faith to be made well, said in a loud voice, 'Stand upright on your feet.' And he sprang up and walked" (14:9–10). Perhaps Luke wants to convey that the apostles' gaze allowed the lame man to see their faith, which awakened his own. The miracle-producing power of the Holy Spirit can be imparted simply through a gaze of faith.

The first part of Peter's response, "I'm broke," shows his faithfulness to Jesus' mission instructions: "Take nothing for your journey, no staff, nor bag, nor bread, nor money" (Luke 9:3). On a human level, Peter had nothing to alleviate the man's suffering, no capacity to help at all. Peter, the once-prosperous fisherman and now highest-ranking leader of the Church Jesus founded, is himself one of the poor. Miraculous healings take place most often by the poor and among the poor — those who have no access to the medical care that money and insurance can provide, no recourse but God alone.

Then Peter committed an act of astounding faith. In the midst of a crowd of people he said aloud, "I give you what I have; in the name of Jesus Christ of Nazareth, walk" (3:6). As if that were not enough, he grasped the crippled man's hand and raised him up. There is no turning back from such an act. Either there will be a miracle or one will appear a complete fool. Peter had such confidence that the Lord would come through for him that he was willing to put his reputation on the line.

The legs of the man, who was more than forty years old and lame from birth (3:2; 4:22), would have been not only congenitally disabled but atrophied from a lifetime of disuse. It is not surprising that he needed a boost to be able to respond to Peter's shocking command. But significantly, it was *not before but after he stood up* that "his feet and ankles were made strong." He had to do the impossible (with Peter's help), before the impossible became possible. As often happened in the ministry of Jesus, the act of faith opened the way for the miracle.

Luke describes the thrilling scene that ensued. "Leaping up he stood and walked and entered the temple with them, walking and leaping and praising God. And all the people saw him walking and praising God, and recognized him as the one who sat for alms at the Beautiful Gate of the temple; and they were filled with wonder and amazement at what had happened to him" (3:8–10). Tears must have flowed as people watched this man, whom they had known as a helpless cripple, now beside himself with joy. There must have been shouts of praise and thanksgiving to God. Perhaps some remembered God's promise about the messianic age to come: "then shall the lame man leap like a stag" (Isa 35:6).

Up to this point in Acts 3 Luke has portrayed numerous signs of the devotion of God's chosen people.[36] Peter and John, like many other Jews, were entering the temple to worship God. The lame man was apparently cared for by fellow Jews who faithfully carried him to the gate every day to ask for alms. The temple was a place where people were especially inclined to give to the needy, fulfilling God's commands (Deut 15:11; Tob 4:7).

But the stunning cure of the man lame from birth is something new, above and beyond these acts of piety. It is a divine act inexplicable in human terms. It is heaven invading earth — the messianic kingdom made present and visible. Jesus had said to the crowds during his public ministry, "Truly,

I say to you, there are some standing here who will not taste death before they see that the kingdom of God has come with power" (Mark 9:1). Before the eyes of the crowd at the Beautiful Gate, his words are being fulfilled.

Proclaiming Jesus the Healer

Peter now has to explain to the quickly burgeoning crowd what just happened and what it means. He takes the opportunity to proclaim the kerygma, the good news of salvation in Christ, and invite people to repentance and faith. He says, in effect, "You've just seen a miracle. Now let me explain who did it and what that has to do with you." Peter's response sets an example for the rest of Church history. The right follow-up to a miracle done in the name of Jesus is always to seize the opportunity to proclaim Jesus.

Peter's explanation of how the miracle occurred is worded somewhat awkwardly: "His name, by faith in his name, has made this man strong whom you see and know; and the faith which is through Jesus has given the man this perfect health in the presence of you all" (3:16). Peter seems to be repeating himself. But he is concerned to underscore two essential ingredients of this healing.

Jesus' *name*, which in biblical thought means his presence and authority, healed the man. Jesus alone has power to heal.

But it was *faith* in his name that released Jesus' healing power upon this man in this place and time. Although the Lord can heal a person without human intervention any time he wants to, he most often chooses to involve his disciples in his miraculous works. The means by which he involves them is faith.

The stupendous healing at the Beautiful Gate, followed by Peter's speech explaining what had happened, has an immediate result: "Many of those who heard the word believed;

and the number of the men came to about five thousand" (Acts 4:4). The glorious power of Jesus' name has been publicly manifested, and the Church has grown exponentially.

This healing is only the first of many recounted in Acts. The miracle causes Peter's own faith to grow to such an intensity that he becomes a kind of lightning rod for the Lord's miraculous power. "They even carried out the sick into the streets, and laid them on beds and pallets, that as Peter came by at least his shadow might fall on some of them. The people also gathered from the towns around Jerusalem, bringing the sick and those afflicted with unclean spirits, and they were all healed" (5:15–16).

Peter's ministry is beginning to look more and more like that of Jesus. At Lydda, Peter finds a man who has been paralyzed and bedridden for eight years. He simply speaks a word of command: "'Aeneas, Jesus Christ heals you; rise and make your bed.' And immediately he rose." The result is mass conversions to Christ among the residents of Lydda and Sharon (9:34–35).

At Joppa, Peter prays at the bedside of a dead woman and raises her to life in the same way, with a simple command. His words are curiously similar to those of Jesus in the Gospel: "Tabitha, rise" (Acts 9:40; see Mark 5:41). This miracle too has an immediate impact on evangelization: "it became known throughout all Joppa, and many believed in the Lord" (9:42).

Multiplying Miracles

The gift of healing, given first to Peter and the Twelve, soon began to be diffused among other members of the Church. Stephen, one of the seven deacons appointed by the apostles to administer the care of the needy,[37] "did great wonders and signs among the people" (6:8) before he was martyred. Another deacon, Philip, evangelized in Samaria — a region previously hostile to the gospel (Luke 9:52–53) — and won multitudes to

Christ by the healings he worked. "For unclean spirits came out of many who were possessed, crying with a loud voice; and many who were paralyzed or lame were healed" (8:7).

Soon afterward, the Church's fiercest persecutor, Paul, was transformed by his encounter with the risen Lord on the road to Damascus. Following this encounter Paul was blind for three days, a penitential sign of the spiritual blindness in which he had been living (9:1–3). He was healed by the laying of hands of a believer named Ananias. Not accidentally, Paul's first miracle was to cause temporary blindness to fall on a man who was vehemently opposing the gospel as he once had. This led to the conversion of the proconsul who witnessed it (13:6–12). As Paul and Barnabas preached in Iconium, the Lord "bore witness to the word of his grace, granting signs and wonders to be done by their hands" (14:3). In the course of his missionary journeys Paul cured a lame man (14:8–10), cast out a clairvoyant spirit from a slave girl who was being exploited (16:16–18), restored a young man to life (20:7–12), and healed a man of fever and dysentery (28:8–9). Paul's most fruitful ministry was in Ephesus, where "God did extraordinary miracles by the hands of Paul, so that handkerchiefs or aprons were carried away from his body to the sick, and diseases left them and the evil spirits came out of them" (19:11–12).

Jesus had promised his disciples at the Last Supper, "Truly, truly, I say to you, he who believes in me will also do the works that I do; and greater works than these will he do, because I go to the Father" (John 14:12). In the miracles worked by Peter and Paul there is already an initial fulfillment of this promise. The Gospels nowhere record Jesus healing people simply by his shadow falling on them or by having his handkerchiefs brought to the sick, nor bringing about mass conversions.[38] Yet Peter and Paul do. As Luke emphasizes, it is not the apostles themselves but the risen Lord Jesus who is acting through them, continuing in them all that he "began to do and teach" during his earthly life (Acts 1:1; cf. 14:3).

There is an important detail that often goes unnoticed in the reports of the disciples' healings in Acts: Luke never says they prayed for healing, with the exception of Peter praying for Tabitha to be raised from the dead and Paul praying for the sick father of Publius (9:40; 28:8). In every other instance, they healed by *announcement* or by *command*, sometimes with the laying on of hands (9:17; 28:8):

"In the name of Jesus Christ of Nazareth, walk" (3:6).

"Aeneas, Jesus Christ heals you; rise and make your bed" (9:34).

"Brother Saul, the Lord Jesus ... has sent me that you may regain your sight" (9:17).

"Stand upright on your feet!" (14:10).

"I charge you in the name of Jesus Christ to come out of her" (16:18).

"Do not be alarmed, for his life is in him" (20:10).

In all these cases, they healed not by asking the Lord to heal, but by boldly exercising the authority the Lord had already delegated to them.

This pattern invites us to consider whether Christians today fully understand the authority we have in Christ, a share in his own divine authority over sickness and all the forces of evil that oppress human beings. Jesus did not say "Pray for the sick" (although James 5:16 does instruct us to do so); he said, "Heal the sick." This command was initially given to the Twelve, to whom Christ entrusted his authority over the Church in a unique and preeminent way. But there are no grounds for confining the command to heal to the Twelve (and their successors, the bishops), any more than we can limit the command to evangelize to bishops only.

Signs and Wonders and the Spread of the Word

It is easy to forget what an outlandish message the apostles had to preach. Jesus, a poor Jewish carpenter from the backwater village of Nazareth, just recently executed as a criminal by means of the Empire's most extreme and degrading form of capital punishment, is risen from the dead and is the long-awaited Messiah and Lord of the whole universe! The gospel sounded no less absurd in the first century than it does today. What is amazing is not that some did not believe, but that anyone believed at all. They did so because of the gospel's own self-authenticating power — its power to make present the reality it announces — and also through the miraculous healings by which God himself bore witness to the spoken message and disposed the hearts of the listeners to believe it.[39]

Luke underscores again and again the relationship between miracles and the growth of the Church. In Jerusalem "many signs and wonders were done among the people by the hands of the apostles.... And more than ever believers were added to the Lord, multitudes both of men and women" (5:12–14; cf. 2:43–47). When Philip evangelized in Samaria, the people gave heed to his preaching "when they heard him and saw the signs he did" (8:6). The extraordinary miracles worked by Paul in Ephesus became known throughout the region, and "fear fell upon them all; the name of the Lord Jesus was extolled ... and the word of the Lord grew and prevailed mightily" (19: 17, 20).

The growth of the Church hardly went smoothly, however. It encountered many forms of opposition, human and spiritual. The early Christians experienced their first taste of persecution when Peter and John were arrested, then forbidden by the Sanhedrin to teach in the name of Jesus (4:18). It was a demand to privatize faith, to stop speaking publicly about the gospel and its implications, not unlike what Christians experience in many parts of the world today.

The believers' response is instructive. They gathered to pray, realizing that intercessory prayer is essential for the success of the Church's mission. Surprisingly, they did not pray for the Lord to overthrow their persecutors, or even for themselves to be kept safe. Rather, they prayed for *even more confidence* to preach the gospel accompanied by supernatural signs. "Lord, look upon their threats, and grant to your servants to speak your word with all boldness, while you stretch out your hand to heal, and signs and wonders are performed through the name of your holy servant Jesus" (4:29–30).

Times of greater trouble require a greater release of the Holy Spirit: greater zeal for the gospel, greater faith to move mountains, more healings, more joy, more courage in the face of persecution. If the Church, feeling external pressures against its evangelistic mission, boldly prayed for signs and wonders then, how can we not do so today?

When they finished praying, "the place in which they were gathered together was shaken; and they were all filled with the Holy Spirit and spoke the word of God with boldness" (4:31). It is a kind of replay of Pentecost, a fresh outpouring of power from on high to meet the new challenges of the day. The Lord has more than answered their prayer.

Not Eloquence but Power

The letters of Paul, written earlier than Acts, give further insight into the role of healings and miracles in the early Church. For Paul, manifestations of the Spirit's power were an essential part of the preaching of the gospel. Although he was capable of eloquent arguments, he deliberately refrained from them so as to preach the unvarnished kerygma, the message of Christ crucified and risen.[40] In fact, Paul believed there was a grave danger in people coming to Christ on the fragile basis of human persuasiveness rather than the firm basis of God's power. Reason can provide a support for faith, but it cannot produce faith itself. So Paul insists, "My speech and my message were not in plausible words of wisdom, but in demonstration of Spirit and power, that your faith might not rest in the wisdom of men but in the power of God" (1 Cor 2:4–5). By "demonstration of Spirit and power" he probably meant both the convincing power of the Holy Spirit at work in the hearts of the hearers, convincing them that the gospel is true, and the miracles that accompany the gospel, proving that Jesus is indeed alive and at work in the world.

Paul regards miracles as the credentials given by Christ to confirm his apostolic calling. He reminds the Corinthians that when he evangelized them, "The signs of a true apostle were performed among you in all patience, with signs and wonders and mighty works" (2 Cor 12:12). He is deeply aware that his missionary success is not due to his skill but to Christ's power working through him. "I will not venture to speak of anything except what Christ has accomplished through me to bring the Gentiles to obedience — by word and deed, by the power of signs and wonders, by the power of the Spirit of God" (Rom 15:18–19).

Reflecting on what Scripture reveals about the earliest stages of the Church's mission prompts the question: Have we taken seriously enough Jesus' injunction to wait until we are "clothed with power from on high"? Do we pray for and seek the manifest power of the Holy Spirit, or do we sometimes initiate evangelistic efforts relying on human plans and human resources rather than divine power? Have we sufficiently attended to the biblical insistence that faith is born not by persuasive reasoning but by the "demonstration of Spirit and power"?

CHAPTER FOUR

Healing in Church History

*They went forth and preached everywhere, while the
Lord worked with them and confirmed the message by
the signs that attended it.*

— Mark 16:20

She was a wealthy and prominent Catholic, and she was in the final stages of breast cancer. Despite the best medical care that money could buy, her disease had advanced and her doctor had informed her that even with an emergency mastectomy, she had only weeks left to live.

But, refusing to give up hope, she turned to God in fervent prayer. It was Lent, and Holy Week was approaching. One night she had a vivid dream in which she was given specific instructions. She was to go to church for the Easter Vigil Mass — the high point of the liturgical year, during which catechumens are baptized — wait for the first woman to come up from the baptismal font, and ask this newly-born Christian to make the sign of the cross over the cancerous breast.

She followed the instructions, and was immediately and totally healed. After a medical examination confirmed that she was now in perfect health, her stunned physician asked what remedy she had used, eager to discover the wonder drug. But when she told him what had happened, he answered in a smug and contemptuous tone, "I thought you would tell me something significant." Appalled at his indifference, she rebutted, "Is it a hard thing for Christ to heal cancer, when he raised a man who had been dead for four days?"

A local bishop later got wind of her healing, and was indignant that so great a miracle, done for such a well-known person, had not been widely publicized. He decided to give her a talking-to. When he broached the subject, she protested that she had not kept completely silent about her healing. So he asked some of her closest acquaintances if they knew about it. They did not. "See what your 'not keeping silent' amounts to," he chided her, "since not even your friends know about it." Then he made her tell the whole story, from beginning to end, while the other women listened in amazement and glorified God.

The bishop was St. Augustine of Hippo, one of the greatest theologians in Church history. The woman was named Innocentia, and the year was about A.D. 400.

Telling the Glad News

Augustine himself tells the story of Innocentia's healing in his book *The City of God*, ensuring that thousands of readers would come to know of this miracle. The story is significant for several reasons. First, it illustrates the importance of testifying to the wonderful works of God. Augustine was rightly indignant that Innocentia had been reticent about her healing. Why? Because he realized that telling others about Christ's miracles gives glory to God, stirs up faith, and moves people to praise and thanksgiving, as it did for Innocentia's friends. Although there are sometimes legitimate reasons to refrain from publicizing a healing — for instance, in the case of some particularly sensitive conditions, or where it is not yet clear whether a healing has occurred — in most cases, it is right to give glory to God by telling others the marvelous things he has done. We should not hold back for fear of drawing too much attention to ourselves. As the psalmist exclaims,

I have told the glad news of deliverance
in the great congregation;

behold, I have not restrained my lips,
    as you know, O LORD.
I have not hidden your saving help within my heart,
    I have spoken of your faithfulness and your salvation;
    I have not concealed your steadfast love and your
        faithfulness
    from the great congregation. (Ps 40:9–10)

Second, Innocentia's story shows that miracles can be done by ordinary Christians — in this case, by a brand-new Christian. What is necessary is not a special gifting, although the Lord does indeed give charisms of healing, but simply faith in the name of Jesus and the power of the Holy Spirit whom we receive in baptism. The unnamed woman who made the sign of the cross over Innocentia had had no time to develop spiritual gifts. But she had just been washed clean of sin and filled with the Holy Spirit. She must have been overflowing with faith as she came up from the baptismal waters, and had no doubt in her mind that Jesus her Savior and Lord had power to conquer cancer.

Christ the Physician

This account from Augustine is just one of hundreds that have come down to us from the age of the Fathers (roughly A.D. 100–600), demonstrating the abundance of healings that continued to occur in the post-apostolic Church.

For the early Christians, healings were not something marginal to the life of the Church. They were at the very heart of God's work of salvation, which is in essence a work of healing. One of the early Christians' favorite images was that of Jesus the great Physician. It appears in the preaching of bishops, in works of apologetics, in liturgical prayers, and in popular piety. St. Ignatius of Antioch writes, "There is only one physician, who is both flesh and spirit,... Jesus Christ our Lord."[41]

Origen speaks of Jesus as the Physician sent by God to heal humanity: "He was the supreme doctor who could cure every infirmity and pain. His disciples as well, Peter and Paul, and also the prophets, are all physicians, as are all those who have been set up in the Church since the time of the apostles."[42]

St. Cyril of Jerusalem, preparing new believers for baptism, encouraged them to come to Jesus with great faith for both physical and spiritual healing:

> Jesus means in Hebrew "Savior," but in the Greek tongue "Healer," since he is physician of souls and bodies, curer of spirits, curing the blind in body and leading minds into light, healing the visibly lame and guiding sinners' steps to repentance, saying to the crippled, "Sin no more" and "Take up your pallet and walk" (John 5:8, 14). For since the body was crippled for the sin of the soul, he ministered first to the soul that he might extend the healing to the body. If, therefore, anyone is suffering in soul from sins, here is the Physician for him; and if anyone here is of little faith, let him say to him, "Help my unbelief" (Mark 9:24). If anyone is encompassed also with bodily ailments, let him not be faithless but draw near, for to such diseases also Jesus ministers, and let him learn that Jesus is the Christ.[43]

The Fathers often spoke of Christ's physical healings as a sign of his deeper spiritual healing of the wounds of sin and death. However, they did not downplay physical healings as if bodily health were of no consequence. Rather, it was Gnosticism and other heresies that devalued the body. As St. Clement of Alexandria insisted, "The Word of the Father, who made man, cares for the whole nature of his creature. The all-sufficient Physician of humanity, the Savior, heals both body and soul."[44]

The Fathers taught that Christ heals us not by a mere decree from heaven, but by taking our infirmities upon himself. He assumed our human nature so as to heal it from within. It is not that he *became* sick, just as in taking on our sins he did not *commit* sin, yet he cured our wounds by transferring them onto himself.[45] As Augustine says: "He, the Lord Jesus Christ himself, is the complete physician.... There on the cross he cured our wounds, where he endured his own for so long; there he healed you from eternal death where he stooped to die in time."[46]

Equipment for Evangelization

For the Fathers, healings are part of the normal equipment that believers are given for evangelization, since evangelizing is not just passing on information about Jesus but communicating his divine life and power. The testimonies from the early centuries indicate that healings, prophecies, exorcisms, and other manifestations of God's power were common, especially in evangelistic settings. These supernatural works were a significant factor in the exponential growth of the Church in the first four centuries.[47] Exorcisms by Christians, for example, were so frequent and so effective that St. Justin Martyr (c. A.D. 100–165) could speak of them as irrefutable evidence for the truth of the gospel. Justin wrote in his *Second Apology*, addressed to the Roman Senate:

> Jesus was born by the will of God the Father for
> the salvation of believers and the destruction of
> demons. And now you can learn this by what
> you see with your own eyes. For throughout the
> whole world and in your city [Rome] there are
> many demoniacs whom all the other exorcists,
> sorcerers and magicians could not heal, but
> whom our Christians have healed and do heal,

disabling and casting out the demons who possessed them in the name of Jesus Christ who was
crucified under Pontius Pilate.[48]

Often it was ordinary Christians who did miracles as
they spread the gospel. As Origen (c. A.D. 184–253) pointed
out, Christ's grace is all the more manifest when miracles are
done in his name by the simplest of people. Christians cast out
demons, he said,

> without the use of any curious arts of magic, or
> incantations, but merely by prayer and simple
> adjurations which the plainest person can use.
> Because for the most part it is uneducated per-
> sons who perform this work, thus making mani-
> fest the grace that is in the word of Christ and the
> despicable weakness of demons, which, in order
> to be overcome and driven out of the bodies and
> souls of men, do not require the power and wis-
> dom of those who are mighty in argument or
> most learned in matters of faith.[49]

St. Irenaeus (c. 115–202) too spoke of supernatural works
done by believers as a cause of the conversion of many to Christ:

> Those who are in truth his disciples, receiving
> grace from him, perform miracles in his name
> so as to promote the welfare of others, accord-
> ing to the gift which each one has received from
> him. For some do certainly and truly drive out
> devils, so that frequently those who have been
> cleansed from evil spirits both believe in Christ
> and join themselves to the Church. Others have
> foreknowledge of things to come: they see vi-
> sions and utter prophecies. Still others heal the
> sick by laying their hands upon them, and they
> are made whole. Yes, moreover, the dead have

even been raised up, and remained among us for
many years.[50]

Seeing sick bodies healed in the name of the Lord Jesus
was a powerful sign to pagans that they no longer had to live
in the darkness, despair, and disorder to which they had been
captive. There was a God who loved them! There was a Savior
who could set them free. People flocked to Jesus, the humble
and merciful divine Physician.

Supernatural Gifts Given at Baptism

How did believers obtain these supernatural gifts for evangelization? The normal expectation in the early Church was that
they were imparted through the rites of Christian initiation.[51]

The process of preparing adults for baptism could last
as long as two or three years. It began when a person came to
initial faith in Christ, usually by hearing the gospel preached,
or witnessing miracles done in his name, or seeing martyrs
shed their blood for his sake, or experiencing the love of the
Christians, or all of the above. This initial conversion was followed by the period of the catechumenate. The catechist, often the bishop himself, taught Christian doctrine and helped
the new believers put off habits of sin and prepare for baptism
with great expectancy. The whole process culminated at the
Easter Vigil liturgy, when they were immersed in the baptismal waters, received the laying on of hands or the anointing
with holy oil, and were allowed for the first time to participate
in the Church's sacred banquet, the Eucharist. It was taken for
granted that as the Holy Spirit was poured into the hearts of
these newly-born Christians he would bestow supernatural
charisms, including the charism of healing.

St. Cyprian of Carthage (c. 200–258), for example, mentions the power to heal the sick and cast out demons among
the divine gifts given to baptized believers:

> By that grace [of the Holy Spirit, received in bap-
> tism] we are given power in all purity to heal the
> sick, whether of body or of mind, to reconcile en-
> emies, to quell violence, to calm passions, to rep-
> rimand demons and force them to disclose their
> identity, punishing them with sharp blows until,
> with loud shrieks and struggles, they flee in terror.[52]

St. Hilary of Poitiers (c. 300–368) likewise speaks of
healing as a charism that is first bestowed in baptism and then
grows through exercise:

> We who have been reborn through the sacrament
> of baptism experience intense joy when we feel
> within us the first stirring of the Holy Spirit....
> We are able to prophesy and speak with wisdom.
> We become steadfast in hope and receive abun-
> dant gifts of healing. Demons are made subject to
> our authority.... These gifts enter us like a gentle
> rain, and once having done so, little by little they
> bring forth fruit in abundance.[53]

The Fathers recognized that not all the gifts given
at baptism are exercised right away. St. Basil the Great explained that just as artistic talent is present in an artist but is
only operative when he is actually creating a work of art, so
the Spirit dwells in the baptized but only operates as need requires in prophecies, healings, or other miraculous works.[54]
The gifts become increasingly fruitful as a person grows in
spiritual maturity and puts them to use for the upbuilding of
the Church.

A Decline in Spiritual Gifts

In the fourth century the Church began to witness a decrease
in healings and other manifestations of the Spirit. By the late

fourth century St. John Chrysostom, bishop of Constantinople, declared that "the gifts … have long since ceased."[55] He regarded such a situation as far from optimal. In fact, he looked
back on the age of charisms with nostalgia: in the early days
"whoever was baptized at once spoke in tongues … many also
prophesied; some performed many other wonderful works."
But "the present church is like a woman who has fallen from
her former prosperous days. In many respects she retains only
the symbols of that ancient prosperity."[56]

Why did such a decline occur? Church historians have
proposed several reasons.

First, the legalization of Christianity by Emperor Con-
stantine in the fourth century led to a large influx of converts,
some with mixed motives. Now that there were social advantages to being a Christian, not all the new believers had the
same degree of sincerity or fervor. Consequently there was
a lowering of standards for baptismal preparation. It was no
longer common to expect supernatural gifts like healing to
be received as a normal effect of Christian initiation. In addition, more Christians were being baptized as infants, which
is a great good in itself, but carries the risk that not all will
personally appropriate the grace of baptism as they mature.[57]
Given this new situation, some of the Fathers spoke of an actu-
alization of baptism that must occur later, in adulthood, when
a person takes complete possession of "the power of holy baptism," and the divine life already given overflows in joy and in
spiritual gifts like prophecy, healing, and miracles.[58]

Second, the Montanist heresy, which put an exaggerated emphasis on prophecy and other charisms, led to an opposite reaction. Montanism began in the late second century as
a spiritual revival movement. Its founder, Montanus, claimed
to have received revelations from the Holy Spirit, and urged
his followers to fast and pray to receive similar inspirations.
But he disregarded ecclesial authority and considered prophets as having a higher authority than the bishops. As a result

the movement came to be regarded as heretical.[59] Because supernatural charisms like healing were closely associated with Montanism, orthodox Christian leaders began to distance themselves from all things charismatic. As early as the second century, however, St. Irenaeus warned against such an overreaction: "They are truly unfortunate who, realizing there are false prophets, take this as a pretext for expelling the grace of prophecy from the Church."[60]

Third, some Christians were influenced by Platonic, Manichaean or Gnostic strains of thought that tended to denigrate the body.[61] These worldviews, though they differ in many respects, all regarded the body as a kind of prison that weighs down the soul. Instead of seeing the human body as belonging to the goodness of creation, as Scripture teaches, they viewed it as a liability, or even as evil. Already in the New Testament era Paul had warned against such views (Col 2:16; 1 Tim 4:2–4). This body-soul dualism led many Christians to deemphasize physical healings and overemphasize asceticism and severe mortification of the body. The same erroneous ideas also resulted in a belittlement of marriage as an imperfect form of Christian life, and a portrayal of heaven as a purely spiritual existence instead of life in a resurrected body.

Finally, there was a growing tendency to identify supernatural charisms with special sanctity, beyond what ordinary Christians were capable of. Gifts that had been widely experienced in the early centuries gradually came to be associated only with monks and nuns who practiced strict asceticism. As a result, for lay people to pray for miraculous healing came to be considered a sign of presumption and pride.

But the decline of supernatural gifts was by no means uniform throughout the Church. St. Augustine (A.D. 354–430), who was a contemporary of St. John Chrysostom, at first held similar views. He thought miracles were needed for the initial spread of the gospel in the apostolic age, but had ceased once the Church had reached maturity.[62] But Augustine began

to change his mind when he read St. Athanasius' biography of
the famous hermit St. Anthony of the Desert, who performed
numerous miracles for the needy people who flocked to him.
Later, when Augustine witnessed abundant healings in his
own cathedral in Hippo, he could no longer deny that God
continued to do miracles in the present. In a sermon he exhorted his congregation, "Our Lord Jesus Christ restored sight
to the blind, raised Lazarus to life…. Let no one then, brethren, say that our Lord Jesus Christ does not do those things
now, and on this account prefer the former to the present age
of the Church."[63] In his greatest work, *The City of God*, Augustine reports some of the striking healings he witnessed, like
that of Innocentia recounted above. He explains why he estab-
lished the practice of recording them:

> I realized how many miracles were occurring in
> our own day … which were so like the miracles
> of old, and how wrong it would be to allow the
> memory of these miracles of divine power to
> perish among the people…. It is only two years
> ago that the keeping of records was begun here in
> Hippo, and already, at this writing, we have more
> than seventy attested miracles.[64]

Even in the late patristic age, when healings were no
longer common among ordinary believers, many of the Fathers wrote of such miracles as playing a crucial role in evangelization. The historian Socrates of Constantinople (born c.
380) writes that St. Gregory the Wonderworker, "while still a
layman, performed many miracles, healing the sick, and casting out devils … such that the pagans were no less attracted
to the faith by his acts, than by his teachings."[65] St. Gregory of
Nyssa adds that when the same Gregory the Wonderworker
went to live in Neocaesarea, there were only seventeen Christians there. By the time he died, forty years later, there were
only seventeen people in the city who were not Christian! A

third Gregory, Pope St. Gregory the Great (c. 540–604), re-
corded the miracles done in his time which he considered
indispensable for the conversion of pagans and heretics. The
pontiff was careful to document his sources, usually eyewit-
nesses.[66]

Healing in the Middle Ages

Throughout Church history, healings and other miracles have
been especially abundant during great waves of evangelization or renewal, such as St. Patrick's evangelization of Ireland,
St. Augustine of Canterbury's evangelization of England, the
Franciscan revivals in medieval Europe, and St. Francis Xavier's mission to the Far East. But even after Europe had become
Christianized, healings continued to be a common feature of
Christian life. Medieval Christian literature is filled with accounts of healings and other supernatural phenomena, often
at shrines such as Santiago de Compostela where the sick came
to beg the Lord for mercy. According to one historian, "Events
called *miracula* permeated life at every level … [they were]
closely woven into the texture of Christian experience."[67]

Historians have often dismissed medieval accounts of
miracles because they tend to be mingled with legends or pious
exaggerations. However, at shrines it was common for clerics
to take sworn depositions, often with intense cross-examina-
tion, of those who claimed healings and those who witnessed
them. In recent decades scholars have begun to publish these
depositions, making it more difficult to dismiss all accounts of
healing as entirely fictional.[68]

Miracles abounded during the Franciscan revivals of
the thirteenth century, when humble friars traveled around
Europe preaching fervently and bringing thousands to deeper
conversion. The construction of the medieval cathedrals were
also occasions of extraordinary manifestations of God's power. Here is how Abbot Haimon, head of a monastery in France,

described the supernatural phenomena that accompanied the building of the cathedral of Chartres:

> Who ever saw, who ever heard in all the genera-
> tions past that kings, princes, mighty men of this
> world ... should bind bridles on their proud and
> swollen necks and submit them to wagons which,
> in the manner of brute beasts, they dragged with
> their loads of wine, corn, oil, lime, stones, beams,
> and other things necessary to sustain life or to
> build churches?... When they had come to the
> church, then the wagons were arrayed around it
> like a spiritual camp; and all the following night
> this army of the Lord kept their watches with
> psalms and hymns; then wax tapers and lights
> were kindled in each wagon, then the sick and
> infirm were set apart, then the relics of the saints
> were brought to their relief, then mystical pro-
> cessions were made by priests and clergy, and fol-
> lowed with all devotion by the people, who ear-
> nestly implored the Lord's mercy and that of his
> blessed Mother for the restoration to health....
> Soon all the sick and infirm leap forth healed
> from wagon after wagon, casting away the staff
> on which they had leaned their crippled limbs,
> and hastening without support to render thanks
> at her altar. Blind men see, and thread their way
> with ease; those with edema are relieved of their
> grievous load and lose their fatal thirst.... Why
> should I enumerate one healing after another,
> when they are innumerable and more than man
> can tell?[69]

The Church has continued to experience healings in every age. In the fourteenth century, St. Catherine of Siena healed plague victims and raised her own mother from the

dead. In the fifteenth century, St. Vincent Ferrer crisscrossed
Europe, preaching and doing an astounding number of healings and exorcisms. St. Teresa Margaret of the Sacred Heart,
with a compassionate kiss to the cheek, healed a sister whose
chronic mouth pain had prevented her from participating in
community life. Healings flowed in torrents from saints such
as Francis of Paola, Francis Xavier, Martin de Porres, and John
Bosco.

Closer to our own time, St. Pio (Padre Pio), St. An-
dre Bessette, and Venerable Solanus Casey ministered healing to thousands of people. Mother Frances Xavier Cabrini
did numerous miracles during her lifetime. Thousands have
been healed through the intercession of St. Thérèse of Lisieux
and through the waters at the shrine of Our Lady at Lourdes.
Countless others have received healings through relics of the
saints and the intercession of the saints, through the sacraments, or through simple prayers to God. From the apostolic
age to our own, miraculous healings have been a normal part
of the life of the Church.

CHAPTER FIVE

Are Healings Real?

*"One thing I know, that though
I was blind, now I see."*

— John 9:25

When Damian Stayne, a lay Catholic evangelist from England, led a healing service at Christ the King Parish in 2013, one of those who attended was Nyla Leipold.[70] Although Nyla had suffered from a form of Parkinson's for twelve years, she came without any expectation of healing for herself. Her brother and aunt had also had Parkinson's, and both had died profoundly handicapped. Nyla is a woman of deep faith who had accepted her illness, knowing the Lord had not abandoned her.

But when Damian asked people with spine and movement disorders to raise their hands for prayer, Nyla knew that meant her. As he led the congregation in prayer, her husband, sister, daughter, son-in-law, and three grandchildren laid hands on her and joined in the prayer. Nyla felt a jolt go through her body. "It was like electricity or lightning," she says. "There was absolutely no pain with it, but it was like there was power with it. And then it was just over, but I knew I had been touched by God." Nyla laid down her cane and walked out into the hallway. Later, when Damian asked anyone who had been using a walker or cane to come forward, Nyla's daughter poked her and said, "Mom, that's you."

After testifying to what she had just experienced, Nyla literally danced down the aisles, to the amazement and delight of everyone present. She was one of about two hundred people who reported a healing that night, but hers was particularly striking in that many parishioners knew her well and had watched her health deteriorate over the years.

A few weeks later Nyla went to her neurologist at the University of Michigan for a regular checkup. Walking in without her cane, she told him she had been healed. He did not respond. Then he put her through her usual battery of tests. She recounts:

> As I was put through the various tests, he could no longer find any of the previous manifestations of my illness. Usually the last test would be to have me walk down the hall, stop and turn — I'd usually stumble when I did that — and slowly walk back. Well, this time I ran. I stopped on a dime, turned, and ran back. He had this big smile on his face. He thanked me for me coming in and showing him all that I could do. He said, "I don't get to see anything like this. My patients never get better."
>
> He said I had no need to come back; I was well. He wrote "Dismissed" on my chart, and the surprised receptionist said, "Dismissed?! We never dismiss patients."

For months afterward, parishioners who had been at the service that night would stop Nyla and ask whether she was still healed. Every time she takes it as an opportunity to retell her story and reassure people that God is still working his miracles today.

> For the last six months I've been almost giddy with excitement, awe, unexpected joy as I keep experiencing new things I can do with ease, like eating a salad or a steak without choking, hurrying up a full flight of stairs or back down. My

handwriting is normal now — you can read it. It wasn't before.

I have had a tremendous weight lifted from me. The spasms that sometimes shook my body have stopped, and I don't choke any more. But it's even more than that. I have a new joy, a new kind of hope and trust. I see everything with new eyes. What I want for everyone is to somehow see and believe in God's love and his mercy, God's constant presence, the Father's love for his children.

The Lord not only healed Nyla's body that night, he gave her a deeper revelation of his love. Healings often bring about a far-reaching *metanoia* (Greek for "change of mind" or conversion) in the healed person that affects everyone around them.[71] God's tenderness, his nearness, his fatherly care, comes to be known in a completely new way. This interior change is often as powerful as the physical healing itself.

Miracles and Mighty Deeds

Nyla has the medical records to prove the disappearance of Parkinson's symptoms from her body. But many people who are healed by God do not possess medical proof. In some cases, there had been severe pain or other symptoms but no official diagnosis. In other cases, the healing could conceivably be attributed to natural causes: perhaps the medication finally began working, or the immune system kicked in, or an emotional boost contributed to a physical recovery. In such cases, was there really a miracle?

The way we think of miracles today differs from the ancient Christian understanding. The idea that a miracle always involves the breaking of the laws of nature is a modern one, stemming from the Enlightenment view of the world as a closed system in which God has no involvement. The eighteenth-century skeptic David Hume, who did not believe in miracles, defined a miracle as "a transgression of a law of nature by a particular volition of the Deity, or by the interposition of some invisible agent."[72] But Scripture and Tradition have a broader view: a miracle is any wonderful deed by which God makes his power manifest.[73] In fact the Greek word for miracles, *dynameis*, simply means "deeds of power." Webster's definition expresses this traditional understanding: a miracle is "an extraordinary event manifesting divine intervention in human affairs."[74]

A miracle in the biblical sense, then, can involve natural as well as supernatural causes. It may involve God working through nature in ways that are mysterious and unknown to us. It may include an extraordinary coincidence, such as a chance encounter that leads someone with a rare condition to just the doctor who can help. It may include the interaction of professional therapy with a divine work of inner healing that goes beyond what therapy can do. The book of Sirach expresses this balanced perspective:

> My son, when you are sick do not be negligent,
> but pray to the Lord, and he will heal you.... And
> give the physician his place, for the Lord creat-
> ed him; let him not leave you, for there is need
> of him. There is a time when success lies in the
> hands of physicians, for they too will pray to the
> Lord that he should grant them success in diag-
> nosis and in healing, for the sake of preserving
> life. (Sir 38:9–14)

For the healed person, it is not important whether the healing is medically demonstrable and indisputable. What counts is that they are now made whole. As the man who had been blind said to the Pharisees, "One thing I know, that though I was blind, now I see" (John 9:25). However the healing occurred, it is reason for joy, celebration, and thanksgiving to God.

Catholic tradition does recognize an important role for medical investigation of claimed healings in two special contexts. First, there is the process of beatification (being declared "blessed") and canonization (being declared a saint). When a person is proposed for beatification, the Church regards a miracle done through that person's intercession as evidence of his or her union with God. When a healing is claimed, there is a long and rigorous process of investigation, involving both non-Catholic and Catholic medical experts, to determine whether the cure was a miracle in the strict sense — that is, it has no natural explanation. The cure must be spontaneous, instantaneous, complete, and lasting. An additional miracle is needed for the blessed to be canonized as a saint.

Second, strict medical scrutiny also takes place for healings reported at Lourdes, where millions have come on pilgrimage since the Virgin Mary appeared to St. Bernadette in 1858. When a person reports a cure to the Lourdes Medical Bureau, two medical committees exhaustively examine the patient and all medical records over a period of several years. Of the seven thousand reported healings in the last century and a half, only sixty-nine have received official approval as miracles. The purpose of this extremely stringent process is to prevent false claims that could discredit Lourdes and the Christian faith itself. But it is important to recognize that in formally declaring only a handful of miracles, the Church is *not* denying that the other healings are wondrous acts of God, miracles in the traditional sense.

When someone believes they have been healed by God, then, it is proper to seek medical confirmation insofar as possible, as Nyla did. When we hear testimonies of healing from others, it is proper to accord them the same degree of trust we would in other circumstances. Being people of faith does not mean being gullible and automatically believing everything claimed to be miracle. On the other hand, it does not mean being skeptical of everything claimed to be a miracle in the absence of indisputable proof.[75] When Nyla danced down the aisles of the church without her cane, she and her family did not need a doctor's signature to know that God had done a marvelous work of healing.

Spreading the News

Many people healed by Christ today are reluctant to spread the news. They may feel that talking about their healing would draw too much attention to themselves, or they may be afraid the illness will reappear and then healing — or Christian faith itself — will be discredited, or they may feel awkward that they were healed while others sought healing and did not receive it. Jesus might even seem to endorse this silence with his order to the healed leper, "See that you say nothing to any one" (Mark 1:44).[76] But it is crucial to recognize that Jesus' demand for secrecy, a common theme in the Synoptic Gospels (scholars have dubbed it "the messianic secret"), applies to the time *before* his death and resurrection. Jesus had to guard against being pigeonholed as a wonderworker and letting his miracles be co-opted for worldly political aims (cf. Matt 12:38–40; John 6:15) until he could reveal his true messianic mission: to suffer and die for our salvation.

After the Resurrection, the secret is out: he is the Messiah, the Son of God, who has come in the flesh to heal and save his people. There is no more need for silence. What was said in secret is now to be proclaimed upon the housetops (Matt 10:27). The mission of Christ's followers is to spread the glorious good news to the ends of the earth, and that includes testifying to the healings and miracles the risen Lord continues to do. This is why Paul and Barnabas, as they traveled from Antioch to the mother church in Jerusalem, "related what signs and wonders God had done through them among the Gentiles," giving great joy to those who heard them (Acts 15:12; cf. 15:3). They did not keep silent about the miracles they themselves had performed out of a misguided sense of humility. It was not about them but about Jesus.

Luke emphasizes the human reactions of overflowing amazement and praise. After Jesus healed a crippled woman, "she praised God" and "all the people rejoiced at all the glorious things that were done by him" (Luke 13:13, 17). The blind man who received his sight at Jericho "followed him, glorifying God; and all the people, when they saw it, gave praise to God" (Luke 18:43). Near the end of Jesus' ministry, as he entered into Jerusalem, "the whole multitude of the disciples began to rejoice and praise God with a loud voice for all the mighty works that they had seen" (Luke 19:37). These are the right responses to the marvelous works of God. In the face of a divine healing, to shrug one's shoulders with a ho-hum attitude would be to dishonor God.

Being healed, or seeing another person get healed, is a profoundly moving experience. Yet as time passes the memory of these wonders naturally begins to fade into the background. This is why Paul often exhorts believers to call to mind the mighty works of God that they experienced at the time of their conversion.[77] Augustine too insisted that healings should be told and retold and remembered. Keeping in mind the marvelous things God has done rekindles faith and helps us return to our first love if we start to get lukewarm.

> Remember the wonderful works that he has done,
>> his miracles, and the judgments he uttered,
> O offspring of Abraham his servant,
>> sons of Jacob, his chosen ones! (Ps 105:5–6)

Why Aren't There More Healings?

At a bookstore in Moscow, not long after the Soviet Union had collapsed, I saw a book with the title *Why There Are No Miracles Today*. The book was written by a Christian, and was full of detailed and sophisticated arguments designed to help believers come to grips with the sad fact that there are no healings or other miracles in modern times. The book made me want to laugh and cry at the same time. I wished I could have sat down with the author to share hour upon hour of miracle testimonies I have heard about or personally experienced.

Why aren't there more healings? The best answer to this question is: There are! Miraculous healings are far more prevalent than most people realize. In his magisterial two-volume *Miracles*, biblical scholar Craig Keener documents hundreds of credible contemporary miracle testimonies from around the world.[78] The well-known author Eric Metaxas recently published miracle stories he collected and vetted from people he knows personally.[79] Laura Jamison Wright tells stories from the ministry of Catholics who have a special charism for healing.[80] Extraordinary healings among Protestants are recounted in *Changed in a Moment* and other books by Randy Clark.[81] For healings earlier in Catholic tradition, there are books like *Saints Who Raised the Dead* and *Nothing Short of a Miracle: God's Healing Power in Modern Saints*.[82]

All this being said, it is true that there is less expectation of healings today than there was in the early and medieval Church. Chapter 4 offered some reasons for the waning of healings and other manifestations of the Spirit in the early centuries. There are several reasons for the further decline in modern times.

First, many Christians have been influenced, even if unconsciously, by Enlightenment rationalism. The Enlightenment rejected the Church's claims of divine revelation in favor of reason alone. It held a Deist conception of God: God as the divine watchmaker who set the laws of physics in motion but has had nothing else to do with the world. The result of these ideas was a loss of the sense of the transcendent that has profoundly affected Western culture ever since. People in earlier times had an understanding of the world as pervaded by mystery, filled with the presence and activity of God. Now the world is regarded as a product of the laws of physics, evolution, and pure chance. With such a worldview, it is harder to believe in or expect supernatural healing.

Second, the nineteenth and twentieth-century "demythologization" of the New Testament created a climate of skepticism. Under the influence of the Enlightenment, many modern biblical scholars dismissed the Gospel accounts of miracles as pious legends, invented (or at least embellished) by the early Church. The conclusions of these scholars have now been widely rejected, since as critics pointed out, if you interpret a miracle story starting with the premise that there are no miracles, you will inevitably come up with purely natural explanations.[83] Yet decades of such misguided biblical interpretation have had a detrimental effect on theology, catechesis, preaching, and the faith of ordinary believers. If Jesus did not truly heal the sick or perform miracles in first-century Galilee, how can we expect him to do so today?

In 1870 the Church responded decisively to these modern currents of skepticism at Vatican Council I:

> If anyone says that all miracles are impossible,
> and that therefore all reports of them, even those
> contained in Sacred Scripture, are to be set aside
> as fables or myths; or that miracles can never be
> known with certainty, nor can the divine origin
> of the Christian religion be proved from them:
> let him be anathema.[84]

Third, Catholics have tended to confuse charisms, including healing, with extraordinary mystical phenomena. Catholic writers in the modern period have typically classified miracles and healings in the category of special mystical gifts that are private, given by God solely for the benefit of the individual.[85] They warn of the dangers of desiring or praying for such gifts. This view differs markedly, however, from the biblical and patristic understanding, which regards healing and other charisms as *ecclesial* gifts, bestowed for the sake of serving others and building up the Church, and thus to be desired and sought, as chapter 8 will show.

Finally, a factor contributing to doubt of miraculous healing in every age has been the existence of charlatans, fraudulent healers, healers using occult practices or other spiritually harmful methods, and healers exercising their ministry for the sake of self-promotion or personal gain. The early Church was no stranger to this problem, and Jesus himself warned of it: "False Christs and false prophets will arise and show signs and wonders, to lead astray, if possible, the elect" (Mark 13:22; cf. 2 Thess 2:9). But as St. Paul cautioned, the existence of false charismatic phenomena ought not to lead to the rejection of all charismatic phenomena (1 Thess 5:20–21; 1 Cor 14:39–40). The many abuses of the gifts of the Holy Spirit are undoubtedly part of Satan's strategy to make the faithful neglect these gifts altogether.

Aware of these cultural influences, we can seek to liberate our minds from them. St. Thérèse of Lisieux, one of the greatest saints of the modern era, taught the way of spiritual childhood: a boundless, childlike trust in the Lord and in his love for us. "Truly, I say to you, whoever does not receive the kingdom of God like a child shall not enter it," Jesus said (Luke 18:17). To expect miracles is to be a child before our heavenly Father, letting go of our desire for control and allowing him to surprise us with his goodness.

God Cares about Our Little Fingers

Some healings have a quality of simplicity that reveals something of God's tenderness toward us. The Lord cares even about our little fingers. Such cures would never make it into a record of documented miracles, yet they are no less real and no less significant in the lives of those who experience them.

Patrick and Maggie Stratton found this out one week when they were watching their five grandchildren, ages nine and under, while their daughter and son-in-law were on vacation. All went well until one evening when Patrick and three-year-old Bethany were outside putting the bikes and scooter back into the garage, while Maggie was inside putting the baby to bed. She remembers:

> All of a sudden, I could hear Bethany screaming. My husband rushed her inside, and I could tell by the look on his face that something bad had happened. He had been holding her as the garage door closed, and at the very instant that two of the panels had locked together, she had reached out with her hand and one of her fingers had been trapped in the vise-like grip of the closed panels. It had taken a couple of tries to get the code right so the door would open and release her finger. Bethany continued to scream. The finger looked crushed. I knew we were on our way to the emergency room.
>
> Before leaving we decided to gather everyone around and say a quick prayer over Bethany. The scene was chaotic. When I started to pray in tongues, everyone (including Bethany) burst into laughter.[86] I was puzzled. Why was everybody laughing? All of them had heard me pray in tongues before. Then I remembered reading somewhere that laughter can be a sign of the power and the presence of the Holy Spirit.
>
> When the laughter subsided, the room filled with peace and tranquility. Without a word the three older children turned away and resumed playing. Bethany, now calm and her old self, wanted to get down and play, too. My husband and I stared in amazement as Bethany

colored a picture in her coloring book. We soon realized that Jesus had totally healed Bethany's finger and then wiped away every tear. Thank you, merciful Jesus!

CHAPTER SIX

The Role of Faith

"Truly, I say to you, if you have faith as a grain
of mustard seed, you will say to this mountain,
'Move from here to there,' and it will move;
and nothing will be impossible to you."
— Matthew 17:20

In the spring of 2014 I co-taught a class on spiritual gifts at my
parish, Christ the King in Ann Arbor, along with our pastor,
Fr. Ed Fride. The class included both a teaching component
and a practicum. We wanted the participants to gain experience in asking God for spiritual gifts and then using them for
others. At one of the sessions we asked the hundred or so participants to pair up with someone they did not know well, then
to pray and ask the Lord for a prophetic word for the other
person. Many of the participants were people of prayer but
had never used the gift of prophecy before.

A young woman named Tirienne paired up with a man
she knew only slightly, Bryan Alfonso. Tirienne had suffered
all her life with severe food allergies. In an email to a friend
she recounted what happened that evening:

> You will never believe what happened on Fri-
> day. At the prophecy workshop Bryan gave me
> a prophecy that there would be a significant im-
> provement in my health, which for me was very
> exciting news. I asked him if he knew about my
> food intolerances and allergies, and he said no.

So at the prayer meeting that night, I asked four people to pray with me for healing from my allergies.

Since then I have eaten blueberries, peanut butter, spicy food, olives, ketchup, spinach, balsamic vinegar, cured meats ... the list goes on — and I've had no symptoms of the allergy whatsoever! No swollen hands, feet or eyelids, no rashes, no hives, no abdominal pain, no nothing. I am just alternating between extreme awe, bouncing off the walls praising God and thinking about what I get to eat next (grapefruit? pickles? sausage? tomato sauce?). Everything is so new and fresh. It's like I have new eyes. Praise God! I just can't even handle the joy right now. I called my parents to tell them and my mom is threatening to cook all kinds of craziness when we visit next weekend.

Bryan had enough courage to share with Tirienne what he thought the Lord was saying, even without being one hundred percent certain of it. And his word was sufficient to stir up Tirienne's faith in the Lord's will to heal her, such that she asked for prayer with great confidence. And the four people who prayed over her did so with great faith and fervor. The Lord used all these interlocking acts of faith on the part of brothers and sisters in Christ to do a powerful work of healing. Now more than a year later, Tirienne has remained healthy and allergy-free.

Tirienne's healing raises the question of the role of faith in healing. Is faith necessary for healing? What kind of faith — faith in Christ in general, or faith that Christ will heal this person at this time? If the person is prayed for but does not get healed, does that mean he or she was lacking in faith? If we emphasize the need for faith, will people who are not healed feel condemned for not having enough faith?

"Your Faith Has Made You Well"

"Your faith has made you well."[87] No statement of Jesus is quoted more often in the Gospels.[88] No saying is more characteristic of his healing miracles.

To the woman with a hemorrhage he said, "Take heart, daughter; your faith has made you well" (Matt 9:22; Mark 5:34; Luke 8:48).

To the sinful woman who wept on his feet, "Your faith has made you well; go in peace" (Luke 7:50).[89]

To the one leper who returned to give thanks for his healing, "Rise and go; your faith has made you well" (Luke 17:19).

And to blind Bartimaeus, "Go; your faith has made you well" (Mark 10:52; Luke 18:42).

In variations of this assurance Jesus said to two blind men, "According to your faith be it done to you" (Matt 9:29).

To the centurion with a paralyzed servant, "Go; be it done for you as you have believed" (Matt 8:13).

And to the Canaanite woman with a demonized daughter, "O woman, great is your faith! Be it done for you as you desire" (Matt 15:28).

In each of these instances, Jesus directly attributes his miraculous healings to faith.[90] The sheer frequency of this saying is reason for us to pay close attention to it. But what did Jesus mean? How can he say *"your faith* has made you well"? Doesn't that wording put too much emphasis on the individual's disposition rather than on the Lord himself? Perhaps some of us, on hearing Jesus say this, might be tempted to reply, "But Lord, that's not really accurate. It wasn't my faith that made me well, but *you* made me well." As in many other instances, to take the Gospels seriously is to be challenged in our accustomed ways of thinking.

A contrary instance helps shed light on Jesus' meaning. The Gospels report that when he preached in the synagogue of his hometown, Nazareth, the people's reaction was to "take offense" at him (Mark 6:3). They believed they knew all there was to know of Jesus. He was just the carpenter, the son of Mary, a villager they had grown up with. They did not see anything special in him. It seemed preposterous to them that he was attracting large crowds and claiming to heal the sick. The Gospel states:

> He could do no mighty work there, except that he laid his hands upon a few sick people and healed them. And he was amazed at their unbelief. (Mark 6:5–6)

This passage is startling, in that it seems to place a limit on the power of the Son of God. How is it possible that Jesus *could not* do miracles?

Mark does not mean that Christ's power was limited in itself, but that he chose to make his miracles dependent on human faith. A healing is an encounter between God's power and human receptivity. Faith opens us to God's power, whereas unbelief closes us to it. Even in Nazareth, however, the general lack of faith did not completely thwart Jesus' ministry, since he healed a few of the sick. But perhaps many more would have been healed had their hearts been receptive. Faith is the Lord's door into human hearts, and it can only be opened from within.

Faith Overcomes Obstacles

The Gospel episodes mentioned above are crucial for understanding what faith is and how to grow in it. It is common to think of faith as assent to a proposition: I believe that statement X is true. For example, "I believe that Jesus is able to heal the sick." This is a genuine but limited kind of faith. Even demons believe in God to that degree (Jas 2:19). Scripture shows us that in fact Christian faith has an active, dynamic quality. It is a personal relationship with the Lord in which we are drawing near to him and entrusting ourselves to him. Faith therefore takes risks; it puts itself forward; it strives against obstacles. In the Gospels those who need healing do not sit at home and simply assume that Jesus will come and heal them if he wants to. They (or their loved ones) actively seek him out. In fact, very often people have to *contend* for their healing.

The leper whose story is recounted in Mark 1, for instance, is bold enough to approach Jesus in public, despite the risk of encountering revulsion and reprimands from others.

Bartimaeus, a blind beggar near Jericho, is even bolder. Sitting by the road one day, he hears a commotion and is told that Jesus of Nazareth is passing by (Mark 10:46–52). Realizing that this may be his once-in-a-lifetime chance, he begins to shout: "Jesus, Son of David, have mercy on me!" In response, "many rebuked him, telling him to be silent." To their minds it is highly inappropriate for someone to shout and carry on like that in the presence of such an important personage. Besides, Jesus is at the head of a solemn liturgical procession of devout Jews on their way to Jerusalem to celebrate the Passover. He does not have time to stop for an individual request. To their minds, it is the wrong time and place to ask for a healing.

It is not easy, especially for a person who is already down and out, to keep from buckling under such intense social disapproval. But instead of being disheartened, Bartimaeus shouts all the louder, "Son of David, have mercy on me!" He refuses to let the censure of others keep him from an encounter with Jesus. His cries, in the midst of the large crowd, finally reach the ears of Jesus, who calls him over. The naysayers quickly change their tune: "Take heart; rise, he is calling you" — as if Bartimaeus lacked heart!

Jesus is apparently not disturbed by the interruption; his whole attention is focused on this one needy man in front of him. "What do you want me to do for you?" Bartimaeus replies, "Master, let me receive my sight," and hears the words that he will never forget: "Go your way; your faith has made you well" (Mark 10:51–52).

Borrowed Faith

The four friends of a paralyzed man also have their challenge (Mark 2:1–12). They are determined to bring their friend to the miracle-working rabbi from Nazareth. But unfortunately when they arrive they find a crowd so densely packed around the door that there is no way to get near Jesus. Instead of turning around and going home in defeat, they put their minds to work. Those of us who have heard this story many times can easily lose sight of how preposterous their behavior is. These incredibly resolute men actually hoist their helpless friend onto the roof, break through the tiles, and lower him into the midst of the gaping audience. A disruption of Jesus' sermon, to say the least. Yet it is a powerful image of intercessory prayer. These men simply will not give up; they will not let any obstacle get in the way of bringing their friend into the presence of Jesus.

The Gospels tell us that when Jesus saw *their* faith — implying that it was irrelevant in this case whether the paralyzed man himself had any faith or not — he forgave the man's sins and then healed him. Faith is communal. It is not a purely individual matter but something that belongs to the body of Christ. If I lack faith for healing, I can borrow it from others around me, asking them to pray for me with faith. Whenever people of faith are gathered together in Jesus' name, their faith is not added but multiplied; the faith of each stirs up the faith of others. "If two of you agree on earth about anything they ask, it will be done for them by my Father in heaven. For where two or three are gathered in my name, there am I in the midst of them" (Matt 18:19–20).

Tenacious Faith

When the woman with a demon-possessed daughter begged Jesus for help, she met a still greater challenge: Jesus ignored her (Matt 15:21–28). How many of us praying for healing have sometimes felt the same way, as if our prayers were hitting a brick wall? But this woman was not put off. She kept crying out so persistently that the disciples got fed up and begged Jesus to send her away. He finally responded to her, but only with a refusal: "I was sent only to the lost sheep of the house of Israel." It was not yet the time in salvation history when the Messiah's gifts were to go beyond the borders of Israel; that must wait until after his resurrection.

But she still did not give up. She knelt before him with a simple plea: "Lord, help me."

Jesus' next reply was an even stronger rebuff: "It is not fair to take the children's bread and throw it to the dogs." How easy it would have been at that point for the woman to turn back in deep discouragement, concluding that it must not be the Lord's will to free her beloved daughter from demonic oppression. But this woman simply would not take no for an answer. She even had a comeback for Jesus: "Yes, Lord, yet even the dogs eat the crumbs that fall from their masters' table." She had chutzpah! She also had humility. She put no stock in her own worthiness, only in Jesus' goodness and his power to set her daughter free.

Jesus finds himself unable to resist such faith. Perhaps there was a twinkle in his eye as he conversed with this woman. His apparent refusals were in reality seeking to evoke just such deep faith — the kind of faith he cannot refuse. Far from being annoyed, he is thrilled. "O woman, great is your faith! Let it be done for you as you desire." And her daughter is healed instantly. Her faith has actually accelerated the plan of God. Ahead of schedule, the "children's bread" — the blessings of the Messiah — is given to a Gentile.

Another Gentile, a centurion, likewise expressed both humility and unbounded confidence: "Lord, I am not worthy to have you come under my roof; but only say the word, and my servant will be healed." Jesus was amazed, declaring, "Truly,

I say to you, not even in Israel have I found such faith" (Matt 8:10). At that moment the man's servant was healed.

Both these cases involve healing at a distance. It is a powerful message to all readers of the Gospel: we do not need to have seen or touched Jesus as he walked on earth to experience his healing power.

When Prayer Is Not Answered

If we pray with confident faith, how then should we respond when our prayers for healing, either for ourselves or for someone else, seem to have no effect? The Gospels teach us the appropriate response. Jesus told a parable that puts to rest any notion that if our prayers are not answered, we should give up asking.

> He told them a parable, to the effect that they ought always to pray and not lose heart. He said, "In a certain city there was a judge who neither feared God nor regarded man; and there was a widow in that city who kept coming to him and saying, 'Vindicate me against my adversary.' For a while he refused; but afterward he said to himself, 'Though I neither fear God nor regard man, yet because this widow bothers me, I will vindicate her, or she will wear me out by her continual coming.'" And the Lord said, "Hear what the unrighteous judge says. And will not God vindicate his elect, who cry to him day and night? Will he delay long over them? I tell you, he will vindicate them speedily. Nevertheless, when the Son of Man comes, will he find faith on earth?" (Luke 18:1–8)

Jesus could hardly have used a more striking example: God compared to an unjust judge! If even this corrupt official, who cares about neither justice nor human suffering, cannot resist continual pestering, how much more will the Lord God, who is Justice itself and is full of compassion, answer the pleas of those who continually cry out to him?

I have often heard people say, "I don't want to bother God. I know he has more important things to take care of." But if the Gospel passages above make anything indisputably clear it is that *God wants to be bothered.* Jesus invites us to be persistent and unrelenting in our prayers. God is infinite; there is no limit to the love and grace he longs to lavish on his children, if only we ask. "He who did not spare his own Son but gave him up for us all, will he not also give us all things with him?" (Rom 8:32).

It is also true, however, that as we persist in prayer the Lord will gradually begin to move in our hearts, changing our desires to become more closely aligned with his. Over time he may lead us to pray in a different way. As I've prayed for healing of my severe eyestrain and migraines, for example, the Lord has led me to see deeper layers of healing that are needed. I've been led to make changes in my lifestyle and ways of thinking: less stress, more relaxation, more trust. I've also begun to recognize how much I need an inner opening of my eyes, to "see what the Father is doing" (John 5:19) — to discern how God is moving and act in accord with it. All this is part of the answer to my prayer for physical healing, far beyond what I initially expected.

Even when it seems nothing is happening in response to our prayer, then, the Lord may be accomplishing immense though unseen changes. Often there are hidden spiritual or psychological mountains that need to be removed before a physical healing can take place (some examples will be given in the next chapter). As we persevere in prayer, the Lord is removing these obstacles little by little. We should never yield to a spirit of hopelessness but rather, as Paul counseled, "pray without ceasing, give thanks in all circumstances" (1 Thess 5:17–18).

Faith as a Way of Knowing

When we pray for healing, how can we do so with great faith? A common mistake is to try to work up faith, to do mental gymnastics to force ourselves to believe that a healing is going to occur. But this turns faith into a human work. People who think this way are sometimes shocked and disillusioned when the healing they prayed for does not happen. But in reality, faith is a gift of God to which we yield. It is a relationship of trust and surrender to the Father, Son and Holy Spirit. It cannot be conjured up. Rather, faith grows as we come to understand more deeply who God is and who we are in him.

As an analogy, consider two different elementary school teachers. One walks into a classroom full of boisterous children and tells them to quiet down, but they ignore her. She does not carry a sense of authority. She does not know how to take control of the classroom. She raises her voice. She begins to cajole, then to threaten: No recess! Extra homework! You'll be sent to the principal! But it has little effect. The children know by experience that these are empty threats, and nothing will happen. They continue being disruptive and disobedient.

The other teacher walks into the same classroom and the children instantly begin to quiet down and pay attention. She carries a sense of authority. When she tells them to behave, they know she means business. She speaks with kindness but firmness. She does not need to threaten disciplinary measures except on rare occasions, and when she does the children know the threats will be followed through.

Christians are meant to walk with the kind of confident authority held by that second teacher. We are heirs of the kingdom. The Lord has given us a share in his own kingly rule.[91] Each one of us has a part in Christ's mission to dismantle the kingdom of darkness and make the kingdom of God present wherever we are. We do that in many ways: by serving humbly, by laying down our lives for others, by sharing God's word at every opportunity, by living a holy life in close communion with the Lord so that we emanate the fragrance of Christ, and by doing battle against sickness and every form of oppression through faith and prayer.

The centurion who begged Jesus to heal his servant understood the secret. He said to Jesus, "I am a man under authority, with soldiers under me; and I say to one, 'Go,' and he goes, and to another, 'Come,' and he comes, and to my slave, 'Do this,' and he does it" (Matt 8:8–9). It is the only occasion in the Gospels where Jesus is said to marvel at what someone says to him. This faithful military officer understood that his authority to command came from his being under authority himself. His soldiers respected his authority because he himself respected authority; he knew what it was to obey. He was not building his own fiefdom but obediently carrying out the task delegated to him by the Roman Empire.

So Jesus himself lived his whole life under the Father's authority. "I can do nothing on my own authority;… I seek not my own will but the will of him who sent me" (John 5:30).[92] His unlimited power over demons, diseases, and death flowed from his total surrender to the Father's will. So too for us, our authority over sickness comes from surrender to the will of the Father in union with Jesus, carrying out *his* will to heal and deliver his children.

Faith is a way of knowing. The more we know who Christ is — his absolute lordship over the whole universe, his victory over sin and death won on the cross, his unconditional love for every human being — the more faith we have. That faith is what enables us to pray against sickness and infirmity with confident authority.

"Increase Our Faith"

Observing Jesus over the years, the apostles could not help but notice how significant a role faith played in his healings. One day they said to him, "Increase our faith!" His reply was not what they expected. "If you had faith as a grain of mustard seed, you could say to this mulberry tree, 'Be rooted up, and be planted in the sea,' and it would obey you" (Luke 17:5–6). Instead of simply agreeing to increase their faith, Jesus challenged them to act on the little faith they did have. The point is that no matter how weak our faith, the way to increase it is by stepping out in faith as the Lord leads — by going out of our comfort zone and asking for the miraculous, even at the risk of looking foolish.

On some occasions, before Jesus did a healing or exorcism, he explicitly challenged people to stretch their faith — to believe to a greater degree than they had before. When the man with an epileptic son begged him, "If you can do anything, have pity on us and help us," Jesus replied, "If you can! All things are possible to him who believes" (Mark 9:22–23). Jairus the synagogue official had faith that Jesus could heal his sick daughter, but when messengers came to say his daughter was dead, his hopes were crushed. Jesus called him to a greater faith than he had imagined possible: a faith that Jesus could even raise the dead. "Do not fear, only believe" (Mark 5:36).

When the disciples asked Jesus why they had been unable to drive out the evil spirit from the epileptic boy, he answered, "This kind can only come out by prayer and fasting" (Mark 9:29). In Matthew's version his response is, "Because of your little faith. For truly, I say to you, if you have faith as a grain of mustard seed, you will say to this mountain, 'Move from here to there,' and it will move; and nothing will be impossible to you" (Matt 17:20). These may seem to be two totally different answers, but they are not. Our faith is strengthened by prayer, which leads us into deeper heart-to-heart knowledge of the Lord and his ways. Prayer is in turn empowered by fasting, which strips us of self-reliance and earthly attachments, removing the "static" from our spiritual eyes and ears so that we can perceive divine realities. As we grow in faith through prayer and fasting, we are able to speak and act in closer and closer alignment with what the Father is already doing, just as Jesus did (John 5:19).

The Thorn in the Flesh

Some people believe that before we pray with someone for healing, we should first discern whether it is the Lord's will to heal them. But that is generally not a good idea, for two reasons. First, it assumes that we can reliably discern what the Lord's will is for another person. But apart from those who have a mature charism of discernment, this is not often the case. It can even be presumptuous. Second, it assumes that we should only pray for things we *already* know with certainty to be the Lord's will. But that would severely limit our intercessory prayer, which is contrary to the Church's practice and tradition.

A better approach is to pray with great confidence in the Lord's will to heal, yet leave the outcome entirely in his hands. Keep praying persistently until the healing occurs, or until there is a sense that the Lord is leading you to pray in a different direction, or until the sick person has a joyful and peaceful assurance that their affliction is part of the Lord's perfect plan.

This is what Paul did about his "thorn in the flesh" (2 Cor 12:7). Paul does not say what the thorn was, only that it was sent by Satan to harass him. Was it a physical ailment? a recurring temptation? an opponent who was blocking his ministry and making life difficult? or relationship problems among his apostolic team members? It may have been any of these, or something else. In any case, the important point is that Paul did not simply *assume* that the thorn was God's will. He prayed three times, begging the Lord to remove it. He stopped asking only when the Lord spoke to him about it, giving him great peace that there was a divine purpose to this thorn.

Some people worry that if we pray with great faith for someone to be healed, the person may be deeply discouraged if they are not healed. This objection is often based on a misunderstanding. To pray for healing with confidence is *not to give someone a guarantee or promise that they will be healed.* No one should give such a promise unless they have a prophetic gift that has proven to be very reliable over time, like that exercised by saints such as John Vianney and Padre Pio.

In my experience, where there is no rash promise but simply healing prayer with great confidence, even those who are not healed at that moment leave feeling encouraged and built up. They have a renewed sense of God's love, and they have also experienced the love and care of the body of Christ through others praying over them. Their faith is not dampened but strengthened to continue bringing their request to the Lord.

Very often in healing prayer ministry nothing seems to happen, but the person is healed that night, or the next day, or gradually over the following weeks. At a conference not long ago in Kalamazoo, Michigan, I gave a talk on healing. At the end of the talk I sensed the Lord telling me that he was healing a person with arthritis, as well as some people with other conditions. I shared this word with the audience. There was no time for individual prayer ministry, but my talk was followed by a time of Eucharistic adoration with praise and worship, the whole crowd kneeling in fervent prayer with hands raised to the Lord.

As I walked into the conference site the next morning, I was met by a woman in the lobby, her face beaming with joy. She burst out, "I think I'm your arthritis patient!" She explained that for years she had been suffering from debilitating arthritis as well as fibromyalgia and other conditions. They had seemed to originate during a time she spent several weeks in Africa in the process of adopting her two children. Since then she had experienced excruciating pain daily. But during the talk the previous day, her faith was stirred up, and during adoration she experienced the Lord's presence in a powerful way. That night in bed, she felt a kind of numbness come over her spine, where she usually experienced the most pain. The next morning, for the first time in years, she awoke completely pain free.

"Can I hug you?" she asked, tearing streaming down her cheeks. "This is the first real hug I've given in a very long time."

Overcoming Obstacles

Bless the LORD, O my soul, and forget not
all his benefits, who forgives all your iniquity,
who heals all your diseases.

— *Psalm 103:2–3*

"Whenever you stand praying, forgive, if you have
anything against any one, so that your Father
in heaven may in turn forgive you your trespasses."

— *Mark 11:25*

I had just finished giving a talk on healing at a Catholic high school. As students and faculty were filing back to their classrooms, a few lingered to introduce themselves or ask questions. One, a science teacher whom I'll call Anna, came up and asked for prayer. She explained that she had been out sick the day before, and was still coughing and running a fever. She felt exhausted and was unable to take a deep breath. "I think it might be pneumonia," she whispered, not wanting anyone to know she had come to work that sick. I immediately agreed to pray over her, and asked a couple of other teachers standing nearby to pray with me.

After a few minutes we finished praying. But one of the other teachers, who knew Anna better than the others, leaned over and gently asked, "How about we pray for that other condition too?" Anna hesitated for a moment before replying, "Okay."

She explained that for the past two years she had been hemorrhaging, "like the woman in the Gospel." She took iron constantly to replenish the blood loss. Surgery had failed to resolve the problem, and she was on high doses of a medication that carried severe side effects, but lower doses had not stopped the heavy bleeding. Because of the side effects and risk of stroke, she had tried several times to stop the medication. Once within twelve hours of a missed dose, she had started hemorrhaging so badly it took a hospitalization and several weeks of a large increase in the dosage to get it back under control.

As we began to pray again, I felt led to ask, "Anna, can you think of anything painful or traumatic that happened around the time this started two years ago?" She thought for a few seconds, then said, "Yeah, it was right around then that my husband stopped going to church."

"I think there might be a connection. Your husband abandoned his spiritual leadership in the family, which must have been painful, and then this condition began. Have you forgiven him?"

"Well, I've tried," she said, a little resentment showing in her voice.

I explained that it is important to understand what forgiveness is and what it is not. To forgive someone does not mean saying, "It's okay. It's fine. No big deal," or "They meant well." To forgive is not to minimize or deny an offense. Sometimes it's *not* okay, and sometimes the person did not mean well. But to forgive means I let go of my right to hold the offense against him or her. It is between that person and God. I choose to let God deal with it, since God alone judges with perfect wisdom, justice, and mercy.

I also explained that to forgive is to make a decision of the will, even though our emotions will not necessarily fall into line right away. We cannot always control our emotions, but we can make an act of the will, choosing to forgive with the help of God's grace. We may need to renew that decision again and again, especially when it involves the people we are closest to.

Anna willingly agreed to say a prayer aloud, expressing forgiveness of her husband. We prayed for a few more minutes, asking Jesus to bless and completely heal her as he had healed the woman in the Gospel.

Eleven days later, Anna emailed me to describe what happened.

You and everyone there prayed over me for a while. It was amazing. It was like a warm cloak being pulled over my chest, and it felt wonderful. The feeling lingered.

When you prayed again, the wonderful warm feeling came over my whole body. It was amazing. I really can't describe how wonderful it was!

I stayed in the chapel after to pray. The lights went off. I thanked Jesus, and I told him I believed. And I tried very hard to believe with all of my heart. You see, I am a scientist, and I am skeptical, and I am prideful, and I probably would never have asked such a big thing of Jesus without my friend's prompting. And Jesus spoke to me. He told me, "It will be all right, my daughter," and he nodded his head, right there in the chapel, the Jesus on the crucifix. I couldn't believe it at all. I remember thinking that either I have totally lost my mind, or I am healed.

It is now eleven days later, and I have not taken any medication to stop the bleeding. On the third day, I had a tiny bit of spotting and then no blood at all. I am still in a total state of shock that Jesus would grant me this blessing. While

I know and believe that miracles do happen, I
cannot believe that one would happen to me.

Oh, and by the way, that night of the
healing, I came home without a cough or fever,
and kept taking these huge, deep breaths that
I had been unable to do earlier that day, just to
keep testing it out. I had no pain, nor any cold
any more either.

God is great!

Later that year I heard from Anna again. "I didn't have
any bleeding for about six months after the healing, and then
I started cycling normally. It is wonderful and my health is a
reminder to me to praise God and be thankful. My husband
has not returned to church, but our marriage is better. We are
going to a concert tonight on a date."

Anna's healing raises the question of what obstacles there
may be to a healing, and how we can seek to remove them. Can
unforgiveness be an obstacle? What about sin? What is the relationship between sickness, sin, and forgiveness?

As the *Catechism* explains, the very existence of suffering and death in the world is ultimately due to original sin,
when our first parents disobeyed God and ruptured the relationship they once enjoyed with him (Gen 3).[93] Their wounded human nature, deprived of its original holiness, was passed
down to all their descendants. Since then we live in a fallen
world, subject to illnesses, accidents, natural disasters, and afflictions of every kind.

But is it also the case that sickness is related to *personal*
sin? There are two Gospel episodes that might at first seem to
give a contradictory answer to this question.

"Your Sins Are Forgiven"

First there is the story of the paralytic mentioned in the previous chapter, who was brought to the Lord by his friends

and let down through the roof. On seeing their faith, Jesus does not immediately heal the man. Instead, he pronounces forgiveness: "My son, your sins are forgiven" (Mark 2:5). This statement is what is called a performative utterance: a statement that brings about what it says.[94] As the scribes sitting nearby recognized, Jesus was not merely informing the man that God had forgiven him; he was *effecting* that forgiveness.

"Your sins are forgiven" was surely not what anyone was expecting to hear. But the paralyzed man probably knew exactly why Jesus said it. Jesus was not necessarily implying that sin had *caused* his paralysis.[95] Rather, there was sin in his life, either past or present, that was blocking the healing work of God. We can imagine how this man who had been carrying a heavy burden of guilt felt an indescribable inner release and freedom at Jesus' words. Chains were being broken. When Jesus then said to him, "rise, take up your pallet and go home," he had the faith and inner freedom to be able to obey.

So today, there are occasions where sin or guilt is an obstacle to healing. In some cases, a physical condition itself is a consequence of bad choices. This is common sense on a natural level. A person may have lung cancer from smoking, or health problems due to drug abuse, or injuries due to an accident resulting from irresponsible behavior. Because of the profound interrelationship of soul and body, even some diseases can have a psychological or spiritual cause. Contemporary medicine recognizes that cancer, for instance, can sometimes result from unresolved anger or long-term resentment, which can weaken the body's immune system.

In most cases, the health problem is not directly related to sin, yet sin or guilt can still be a block to healing. The person may feel unworthy to be healed, knowing there is a serious sin on his conscience. Or he or she may have an attachment to some sin, such as using pornography, and be afraid of yielding to the Lord since it would mean having to give up the sin.

If you are praying for someone and sense that sin or guilt is an obstacle, a good approach is to very discretely and gently ask, "I sense that there may be something weighing on your conscience that is an obstacle to healing. Do you think that might be the case?" Allow the person complete freedom to decide whether and how much he wants to disclose. Never coerce or pry for information. If the person says no, then simply continue to pray for healing, and trust the Lord to do whatever interior work he needs to do in his timing. If the person says yes, then invite him to say a simple prayer of repentance (either out loud or silently, as appropriate) and to leave that sin at the foot of the cross. Encourage him to avail himself of the grace and power of the Sacrament of Reconciliation as soon as possible. Then pray for the physical healing.

In some cases a person has already confessed a sin and received absolution, but guilt is still burdening her conscience. In that case it is a false guilt. Remind her of the truth that Jesus has shed his infinitely precious blood for the forgiveness of our sins. How can we not believe his blood is sufficient to atone for all our sin, when God has said that it is? (cf. Heb 9:13–14). "As far as the east is from the west, so far does he remove our transgressions from us" (Ps 103:12). Doubt in the Lord's forgiveness of our sin does not come from God but from the evil one, "the accuser of our brethren" (Rev 12:10). Invite the person to say a prayer aloud, renouncing in the name of Jesus a spirit of guilt and condemnation. Then pray for the physical healing.

Neither This Man nor His Parents

The second Gospel episode, which provides an important counterbalance to the story of the paralyzed man, is the account of the man born blind in John 9. When the disciples saw this man they took the occasion to ask Jesus a theological question: "Rabbi, who sinned, this man or his parents, that he was born blind?" Their thinking was based on an assumption common among some Jews at the time: since Scripture affirms that God blesses the righteous and punishes sinners, an affliction like blindness must be the result of some personal sin.

Jesus rejects that assumption.[96] "It was not that this man sinned, or his parents, but that the works of God might be made manifest in him" (John 9:2–3). Jesus changes their focus from the *cause* to the *purpose* of this affliction: God has allowed it because he is going to do something so wonderful in and through this man that it far outweighs his infirmity. God will not only heal him physically, but open his spiritual eyes to the revelation of Jesus the Messiah. And through him the glorious power of God will be displayed to many others.

Jesus' reply is a warning against any blanket assumption that illness is due to personal sin. This was the error of the well-meaning friends of Job, who tried to convince Job that he must have done something terrible to deserve all his misfortunes. They were soundly rebuked by God (Job 42:7). It is indeed true that illness is *sometimes* due to personal sin. In the Psalms, the sick man's plea for a cure is sometimes linked to a confession of sins: "there is no health in my bones because of my sin" (Ps 38:3).[97] But most of the time this is not the case. Other psalms speak of a suffering righteous man, protesting his innocence before the Lord (Ps 18; 34).

The bottom line is that we are not the ones to judge whether a physical ailment is related to personal sin. God alone is the judge. Even the afflicted person should not presume to judge himself (cf. 1 Cor 4:4). And whether the ailment is related to sin or not, God's mercy abounds for both forgiveness and healing. God does not heal because we deserve it but simply because he loves us. The psalmist who is aware of his sin is just as confident in God's healing as the psalmist who proclaims his innocence. The psalms even teach us to pray, "LORD, be gracious to me; *heal me, for I have sinned against you!*" (Ps 41:4).

For the Lord "forgives all your iniquity, ... heals all your diseases" (Ps 103:2–3).

Intergenerational Obstacles

Another important question is embedded in the disciples' inquiry about the blind man: Can illness or infirmity be caused by the sin of one's parents? Can afflictions be passed on through the generations?

That children often suffer from the consequences of their parents' sins is a fact confirmed by both psychology and human experience. People's physical and mental health status, even as adults, can sometimes be rooted in the behavior of their parents. Patterns of sin or bondage can be inherited. Alcoholism, for instance, or physical or sexual abuse, or emotional disengagement, create dysfunctional patterns that are passed down through the generations. Scripture too confirms this principle. God declares, "I the LORD your God am a jealous God, visiting the iniquity of the fathers upon the children to the third and the fourth generation of those who hate me" (Exod 20:5). This does not mean children bear the *guilt* of the sins of their fathers — a false conclusion that is firmly rejected in Ezekiel 18. Rather, God allows the temporal *consequences* of sin to take their toll on subsequent generations.[98] Such is the interconnectedness of the human family that our sin has a ripple effect, negatively influencing all those around us, especially children.[99]

But all the more does grace! The same passage in Exodus continues, "but bestowing mercy to thousands [or 'to the thousandth generation'] on the children of those who love me and keep my commandments" (Exod 20:6). God allows us to be adversely affected by others' sins only because he is always able to bring a far greater good out of our suffering. "We know that in everything God works for good with those who love him, who are called according to his purpose" (Rom 8:28).

When evidence of such a generational pattern comes to light during prayer for healing, we can ask the Lord to break the unhealthy cycle and heal the wounds caused by it. For example, I recently prayed over a woman who suffered from severe depression. When I asked if anyone else in her family had depression, she affirmed that her mother and grandmother and several other relatives had suffered from it. I asked her to pray a simple prayer, renouncing a spirit of depression in the name of Jesus. I prayed that this generational pattern would be broken and that she would be released from all spiritual bondage related to it. There were also abusive behaviors in her family that probably contributed to the depression. I led her in a prayer forgiving each family member who had hurt her or failed her in some way. Through this forgiveness the Lord released her from deep-seated resentments. Although she will probably have a long road to recovery with professional help, she now knows she is not a helpless victim: she can fight against depression in the authority of the name of Jesus.

How do we know when to pray for generational healing? A sound rule of thumb is to do so only when there is a clear reason to believe the affliction is rooted in generational patterns, as in the example just given. I believe it is reasonable to address patterns that go back as far as one's grandparents or great-grandparents, but no further, in accord with the biblical phrase: "to the third and fourth generation." Generational influences to that extent can usually be confirmed by memory or family history. To go further would be to enter more and more into the realm of what is speculative and unverifiable.

Some of those who practice healing of the family tree claim detailed prophetic insight into curses or other influences from many generations ago, or even centuries ago, that must be removed by specific kinds of prayers. But this practice comes dangerously close to a kind of Gnosticism, in which salvation is dependent on the knowledge to which a person has access. It can also create fears that there may be other un-known generational curses negatively impacting one's life. It can lead to a sense of helplessness and a denial of personal responsibility for one's own actions.

As in all forms of prayer ministry, we should pray with humility, good discernment and common sense. We may have a helpful prophetic insight, but we should never presume it is infallible. Our prayer should be simple, trusting in the Lord to heal whether or not we perfectly understand all the factors that contributed to the illness.

Inner Wounds

Often people need more than a single occasion of healing prayer ministry. They need to be soaked in prayer over weeks, months, or years. Even if nothing seems to be happening, the Lord is working great changes interiorly. In some cases divine "surgery" is needed on the inside before the physical healing can take place, and it does not always happen instantaneously. St. John of the Cross, speaking of our union with Christ in prayer, used the example of a green log thrown on the fire. For a long time it may seem that nothing is happening. But inside the log is getting hotter and hotter, drier and drier. And the moment will come when it suddenly bursts into flame.[100] If our hearts are open to the Lord, every instance of healing prayer brings us closer to that point.

What inner wounds are there that need divine surgery? Many people have difficulty accepting good things from God, a sense of unworthiness or even a deep sense that God will not heal them because they deserve to suffer. They may have a reluctance to believe out of fear of being disappointed. Such people need to be immersed more and more deeply in God's unconditional love.

Conversely, some people have an underlying sense of entitlement that keeps them from being poor in spirit. They may believe God owes them something because of their faithful service to the Church or regular practice of the sacraments. God in his wisdom may withhold a healing that would be spiritually damaging until he works in a person the necessary poverty of spirit that allows them to receive his blessings as they truly are: free, unmerited gifts.

In others, there can be a spirit of infirmity that makes a person identify with his or her illness and even be afraid of healing. Jesus asked the invalid at the pool of Bethesda, "Do you want to be healed?" (John 5:6). That may seem a ridiculous question, until we realize that for some people, illness can become a crutch that enables them to avoid taking responsibility for their life. An infirmity may bring advantages that are not easy to give up: attention, or dependence on another person, or even disability benefits. A person may have become so used to their condition that they are afraid of taking on a new identity as a healed person. They may need faith not only for healing, but also for the Lord to provide all the grace needed for a new way of life.[101]

Unforgiveness

Finally, perhaps the greatest block to healing is underlying unforgiveness of another person. Jesus directly linked the efficacy of prayer to our willingness to forgive: "Whenever you stand praying, forgive, if you have anything against any one; so that your Father who is in heaven may also forgive you your trespasses" (Mark 11:25). Unforgiveness closes our heart to God's grace. Conversely, choosing to forgive can release grace in a powerful way, as it did for Anna in the story at the beginning of this chapter.

To illustrate how destructive unforgiveness is, Jesus told the parable of the unmerciful servant (Matt 18:23–35). The gist of this story is hard to convey in translation. The servant owed his master ten thousand talents, which in our economic

terms is some four billion dollars — an absolutely astronomi-
cal sum! The master represents God, and that debt symbolizes
the measure of how our sin has offended God. Once we realize
the enormity of the debt, we can see how preposterous is the
servant's claim: "Lord, have patience with me, and I will pay
you everything." Despite this nonsensical promise, the master,
filled with compassion, freely writes off the entire debt. This is
what God, in his mercy, does for us.

The servant then goes out and meets a fellow servant
who owes him a hundred days' wages — in our terms, several
thousand dollars. That debt symbolizes the measure of how
we offend one another by our sins. It is fairly sizable; it is not
a negligible amount. Yet it does not begin to compare to the
debt owed to the master. The fellow servant promises likewise
to repay the debt. In this case, the promise is realistic. Yet the
man chokes his fellow servant and throws him into prison.
Why such a hard-hearted response?

The key to this parable is realizing that *the servant was
unmerciful because he would not receive mercy.* He could not
bring himself to accept such an immense free gift from his
master. It was too humbling. Impossible as it was, he still wanted to pay back the debt somehow, so he needed every penny
he could get. That is why he was so desperate to get back what
his fellow servant owed.

This is how unforgiveness functions for us: we have a
hard time receiving God's free gift of mercy, so we begrudge
giving away mercy to others. We hold on to being justified in
our anger, being right and keeping others in the wrong. But
there is a high price to pay for such mercilessness. The parable
ends with the master delivering the wicked servant to the jail-
ers (or "torturers"), until he should pay all his debt. Those who
hold on to grudges are indeed subject to torture interiorly, and
they risk the eternal pain of separation from God. They keep
themselves imprisoned in worse bonds than the person they
resent.

How can we address this obstacle in healing prayer ministry? If it seems likely that a person's condition is related to an offense committed by another, then invite him or her to say a prayer of forgiveness out loud. For instance, "In the name of Jesus I forgive the driver of that car that crashed into mine." "I forgive the doctor who misdiagnosed me." "I forgive my boss for putting so much pressure on me that I became stressed out." "I forgive my mother for criticizing me all the time." We do not need to know with certainty whether the other person is guilty before God or not; that is God's affair. To forgive is to set *ourselves* free, and to allow God's mercy and healing to overflow in us.

Pressing In

Removing the obstacles to healing is itself a profound work of healing. Very often it is followed by a breakthrough in physical healing. If this does not occur right away, we should encourage the person not to give up but to take steps to increase their faith and deepen their relationship with the Lord (for instance, meditating on Gospel passages about healing), and to come back another time for more prayer. Prayer for healing sometimes requires that we keep pressing in, seeking to understand the Lord and his ways, placing our requests before him, even wrestling with the Lord as Jacob did (Gen 32:24–30).

As Pope Francis said:

> Miracles still happen today. But in order to allow the Lord to carry them out we must pray with courage to overcome that "feeling of disbelief" that dwells in the heart of every man, even in men of faith. A prayer that calls for an extraordinary action must be a prayer that involves all of us, as though our very life depends on it…. A courageous prayer, that struggles for that miracle. Not

like those prayers of courtesy: Ah, I will pray for you! Followed by one Our Father, a Hail Mary and then I forget. No! It takes a brave prayer like that of Abraham who was struggling with the Lord to save the city, like that of Moses who prayed, his hands held high when he grew weary.... Not a polite prayer, but a prayer from the heart.... Lord, I believe! Help my unbelief.[102]

CHAPTER EIGHT

The Charism of Healing

*To one is given through the Spirit the utterance of
wisdom,... to another faith by the same Spirit,
to another gifts of healing by the one Spirit.*
— *1 Corinthians 12:8–9*

Tom Naemi is not the kind of person you would expect to
have a healing charism. Nor did he receive it at a likely time or
place. Tom was in the state penitentiary, serving a sixteen-year
term for organized crime, when the Lord began to speak to
him in dreams. Soon afterward, Tom was praying with people
for healing, with miraculous results.

Tom is a Chaldean Catholic who was born in Baghdad,
Iraq, and came to the United States with his family at age elev-
en. Growing up in Detroit, he went to Mass every Sunday and
served as an altar boy. But as he worked in his family store, he
was gradually drawn into a world of corrupt and often violent
competition. Tom had a quick temper, and over time the feud
with his business rivals escalated into beatings, gun chases,
and fire-bombings. The end came when Tom attempted to
blow up his enemy's store. His truck filled with explosives
caught fire prematurely, and instead of getting his hoped-for
revenge, Tom barely escaped with third-degree burns and a
long prison sentence.

In prison, Tom was a man filled with rage, determined
to settle the score once he got out. But as he attended Bible
studies and Catholic services, his heart began to soften. Then
he began to have dreams in which the Lord showed him peo-

ple he wanted to heal. After one dream, Tom used the prison phone to call up a couple he was acquainted with. He told them he knew they were planning to get a divorce, but that the Lord wanted them to stay together. The husband was shocked that Tom knew about it, but still skeptical — until Tom revealed a secret they had never told anyone. The couple agreed to talk and pray with him. They eventually reconciled, and remain happily married to this day.

Switching through the TV channels one day, Tom came across a preacher who was shouting, "Do you know Jesus, or are you just a churchgoer? Have you given your life to Jesus?" At that moment the power suddenly cut out. Sitting on his bunk, Tom was deeply convicted. He prayed, "Lord, you know I tried to run my own life and I made a total mess out of it. I give you my life. From this moment on, I'm going to let you use me however you see fit." He went to confession and repented of all the anger, hatred and vengeance in his heart. In his own words, Tom "went from being a hard man to being like a marshmallow." While attending a Life in the Spirit Seminar,[103] Tom and some friends would go out in the prison yard every day to pray, sing about Jesus, and read Scripture. One day in his cell he felt the Holy Spirit come like a rushing wind, setting his whole being ablaze with fire. He knew the Lord was giving him a special mission. He laid hands on his cellmate, who had an old ankle injury, and the ankle was instantly healed.

After his release in 2005, Tom began leading Bible studies and praying over anyone who came to him in need of healing. Since then many have been healed, including people with breast cancer, kidney cancer, leukemia, blindness, arthritis, colitis, allergies, and severe anxiety.

On one occasion, Tom was leading a healing service at a parish in Windsor, Ontario, when a teenage girl named Katina came up for prayer. She told him she had a chronic ankle sprain and was in constant pain. She had worn an ankle support for four years, was on and off crutches for two years, and was unable to run or even to stand for more than five minutes. Recently she had also suffered a head injury and had terrible headaches. Tom laid hands on her and prayed, "Lord, you know what she needs. In the name of Jesus I speak healing to these bones. I prophesy to them, come alive!" Katina fell and was resting in the Spirit for about twenty minutes.[104] As Tom continued praying over others, suddenly out of the corner of his eye he saw her running down the aisle. Then he saw her father running toward her from the other side of the church; both were sobbing. She came up to Tom saying, "I'm healed!" He replied, "There's the guy with the microphone. You go and give Jesus the glory." She was given the microphone and testified to her healing before everyone in the packed church. She later wrote to Tom:

> During your healing service my head was pounding. The noise and singing were causing severe pain in my head. While waiting in line I had to sit because my ankles and knee were crying in pain. But when you were using God's power to heal me, I immediately felt like I could stand straight without any pain in my knee. When I was out in the Spirit lying on the floor I was crying because I could move my wrist and fingers (side effects from head trauma) without any pain. All my pain had instantly left me. I got up and I went to the bathroom to cry and while walking there I noticed I was no longer limping. I was standing with no pain. A few minutes later I was running and jumping and felt no pain. My headaches were gone!
>
> The next day at school I was so happy and jumpy, my friends asked me what I was on because it had been so long since I was that happy. For five days now, I haven't taken any pain pills. I can concentrate and focus and I'm not in

pain. Thank you so much for being God's instrument to heal me.

On another occasion, a woman who was all skin and bones was brought to Tom for prayer. She was mentally ill and had a wasting sickness that doctors were unable to diagnose. By that point she weighed only 78 pounds. Tom prayed for her. A few months later he received an email from her sister: "I have had the joy of watching her recover.... Today she is vibrant and a joy to be around. She has picked up weight, she is a healthy 130 pounds, involved in her daily activities and smiles a lot. We had not seen her true smile in twenty years."

Healing and Holiness

Tom is clearly someone to whom the Lord has given an extraordinary charism of healing. But how is it, we might wonder, that God would give such a charism to a convicted mobster, even before he was fully converted? Aren't there plenty of people more worthy? As in so many areas of life, so also with charisms God overturns human ways of thinking. God does not give his gifts to those who are worthy. He gives them as free gifts to the *undeserving*, which includes all of us.

The very word "charism," the New Testament word for a gift of the Spirit, conveys this. It means *freely bestowed gift*, unmerited favor. Paul lists healing as one of these charisms that are graciously distributed by the Spirit (1 Cor 12:9). The charisms are not a reward for virtue (cf. Gal 3:5). They are not a sign of heroic sanctity. God gives them freely, simply because he loves his children and delights to involve them in his work of building up the body of Christ.

In fact, Scripture strongly rejects the idea that healings are a measure of holiness. Peter, after healing the lame man at the temple gate, admonishes the bystanders, "why do you look so intently at us as if we had made him walk by our own power or piety?" (Acts 3:12). We can easily agree that Peter did not do this miracle by his own power, since Christ alone has the power to heal. But Peter also insists that his *piety* had nothing to do with it. Peter is keenly aware of his own unworthiness. He well remembers the moment of his deepest failure, not so long past, when he denied his Lord (Luke 22:56–62). He has been stripped of illusions about himself (cf. Luke 22:33–34). But having been filled with the Holy Spirit at Pentecost, he has become a generous receiver of the gifts of God. He is overflowing with the power and love of the risen Lord, and he is eager to give away what he has received.

Jesus too cautions against the assumption that charisms, even extraordinary ones, are a proof of holiness. He warns, "Many will say to me on that day, 'Lord, Lord, did we not prophesy in your name? Did we not drive out demons in your name? Did we not do miracles in your name?' Then I will declare to them solemnly, 'I never knew you. Depart from me, you evildoers'" (Matt 7:22–23). There is no reason to think Jesus is referring to false prophecies and miracles. Rather, these are real gifts, freely bestowed by God, but misused by the recipient for selfish purposes instead of God's purposes. The sobering truth is that it is possible to exercise supernatural gifts and yet have a heart hardened against the Lord (1 Cor 13:1–3). Even the high priest Caiaphas, who led the charge seeking to put Jesus to death, prophesied without knowing it (John 11:49–51).

That being said, it is also true that God is looking for those who are thirsty for him, who are so passionate for his glory that they are willing to be totally surrendered to him. "For the eyes of the LORD range throughout the entire earth, to show his might for those whose heart is true to him" (2 Chr 16:9). God is looking for those who will give him an unqualified *yes*: "Lord, I will go wherever you send me. I will do whatever you call me to do. Only use me for your glory." He seeks out those who think nothing of their own merit or qualifications, but who ardently desire to be an instrument of his love. "God chose what is weak in the world to shame the strong, God chose what is low and despised in the world, even things that are not, to bring to nothing things that are, so that no human being might boast in the presence of God" (1 Cor 1:27–29).

So it is not only saints to whom God gives charisms like healing. Still, should ordinary people seek or expect such charisms? The answer is found in St. Paul's teaching on the gifts of the Spirit, where he explains how they function in the life of the Church.

Paul's Teaching on Charisms

Paul's most extensive teaching on the charisms is in 1 Corinthians, a letter filled with practical instruction on the life of the local church. It is evident that the Corinthians were richly endowed with spiritual gifts (1 Cor 1:5–6); however, they were also immature and divisive, which was hindering them from using these gifts effectively. Paul encourages them in the use of the gifts, but teaches them how to do so in right order. Chapter 12 of the letter explains the source and purpose of the gifts; chapter 14 gives detailed practical directions on using them. In the middle is chapter 13, Paul's great hymn to love. Far from being a digression, the chapter on love provides the foundational principle that orders all exercise of the charisms.[105]

What are charisms? First, it is important to distinguish them from another kind of gift mentioned in Scripture. The prophet Isaiah foretells that the Messiah will be endowed with seven qualities bestowed by the Spirit: wisdom, understanding, counsel, fortitude, knowledge, piety, and fear of the Lord.[106] Catholic tradition has come to call these the seven *sanctifying gifts* of the Spirit. They are given to every Christian at baptism and confirmation, and their purpose to make us holy, forming in us the character of Jesus the Messiah.[107]

The *charismatic gifts* or charisms, in contrast, are distributed by the Spirit in different measures to different people. They are not primarily for personal sanctification but for building up the body of Christ.[108] They are by definition gifts that are to be given away, gifts to be used for others. The charisms help free us from individualism and learn to be dependent on one another, so that the body of Christ functions as a living organism, each part contributing in a unique way to the whole. Paul writes, "If the whole body were an eye, where would be the hearing? If the whole body were an ear, where would be the sense of smell? But as it is, God arranged the organs in the body, each one of them, as he chose.... The eye cannot say to the hand, 'I have no need of you,' nor again the head to the feet, 'I have no need of you'" (1 Cor 12:17–21). No one has all the charisms, precisely because we need one another.

Charisms are also distinct from human talents. A charism is not a natural ability but a *supernatural* gift of the Holy Spirit. It either enables one to do what is humanly impossible (such as prophecy or healings) or elevates a natural endowment (such as teaching or hospitality) to a supernatural level of efficacy for building up the body of Christ. Paul lists some of the more obviously supernatural gifts like healings, prophecy, and miracles in 1 Corinthians 12:8–10.[109] In other passages he lists gifts that seem more ordinary but are no less important: service, teaching, exhortation, contribution, administration, and acts of mercy (Rom 12:6–8).

Paul also refers to charisms as "manifestations of the Spirit" (1 Cor 12:7). That means that every time you exercise a charism, God the Holy Spirit is operating through you, displaying his presence and power. A charism like healing is not something you "possess" or can pull out of your pocket at will. You cannot heal someone whenever you feel like it. Rather, you are a musical instrument on which the Holy Spirit plays according to his will and his timing. The more yielded you are to him, the more freely he will play.

Paul insists that every Christian is endowed with one or more charisms for building up the body of Christ. "To *each* is given the manifestation of the Spirit for the common good" (1 Cor 12:7; cf. Eph 4:7). Every Christian has an irreplaceable role to play in the Church's mission; each is given charisms that perfectly correspond to his or her unique role. The use of our charisms is therefore not optional. God's gifts bring a corresponding responsibility to use them: "As each has received a charism, *use it* to serve one another, as good stewards of God's varied grace" (1 Pet 4:10; cf. Rom 12:6–7). Many people do not exercise charisms because they have no idea that they even have them. But this is a great loss to the body of Christ. It is a major reason for the weakness of many efforts at evangelization and parish renewal.

Asking for Gifts

Paul exhorts Christians not only to use the gifts they already have, but to *strive eagerly for* the spiritual gifts, especially those that are most useful (1 Cor 14:1). The Greek verb for strive eagerly, *zēloute*, can also be translated "earnestly desire" or "be zealous for." But how can we strive for them if they are gifts? God gives them freely, but we can pray for them, learn about them, stir them up, put them into practice, grow in their exercise. The charisms are not static. Although the Holy Spirit distributes them as he wills, he works most fully through open and generous hearts — people who are willing to step out in faith and boldly exercise their charisms for the good of others, even if they will make some mistakes along the way. The gifts grow in power and purity as we grow in our relationship with God.

Paul asks, "Do all work miracles? Do all possess gifts of healing?" with the obvious rhetorical answer "No" (1 Cor 12:29–30). Some interpret that passage to mean that most of us should not expect to be used for healing, since the charism of healing is only given to some. But it cannot mean that, since the only way to find out if you have the charism of healing is to pray for healing. More importantly, immediately after those rhetorical questions is Paul's exhortation quoted above: "Strive eagerly for the greatest spiritual gifts," implying that we can and should ask for charisms we do not yet have if they would serve the mission of the Church.

Whoever is living as a committed disciple of Jesus should therefore not be afraid to ask for the gift of healing, provided there is no hidden selfish agenda. Why ask for it? Simply because there are people who need to be healed, people who are broken and hurting and who badly need to experience God's love. The risen Lord is waiting for his disciples, filled with the Holy Spirit, to act in the power they have already been given and to ask for more heavenly power to meet the needs of those around them. You do not need to begin by asking for a permanent gift, just the gift of healing *for this one person* with whom you are praying at this moment.

And a word of advice: if you are serious about wanting the gift of healing, ask for humility at the same time, and then expect God to arrange circumstances in your life that will very effectively answer that prayer!

God loves to lavish his gifts on the simplest and lowliest of people, people who put no stock in themselves, because then it is clear that the glory belongs to him alone. St. Francis Xavier, the great Jesuit missionary to the Far East, tells of what he did in India when he was so besieged with requests to visit the sick that he could not keep up.

> It was impossible for me myself to satisfy all
> … so I hit on a way of serving all at once. As
> I could not go myself, I sent round children
> whom I could trust in my place. They went to
> the sick persons, assembled their families and
> neighbors, recited the Creed with them, and
> encouraged the sufferers to conceive a sure and

well-founded confidence of their restoration. Then after all this, they recited the prayers of the Church. To make my tale short, God was moved by the faith and piety of these children and of the others, and restored to a great number of sick persons health both of body and soul. How good He was to them! He made the very disease of their bodies the occasion of calling them to salvation, and drew them to the Christian faith almost by force.[110]

By using these children to heal, the Lord gave a powerful message to the people of India whom Francis was evangelizing: you do not need to be a European missionary to be an instrument of God's healing power. You do not need to be a priest, or a scholar, or a saint. You just need a heart filled with simple, childlike faith in the Lord Jesus.

At the center of Paul's teaching on the charisms is his hymn to love in 1 Corinthians 13. Every use of charisms, including healing, is measured by the standard of love. The sobering truth is that even the most extraordinary charisms are nothing, utterly worthless, apart from love (13:1–3). When used for selfish purposes, such as self-promotion or financial gain, they even become spiritually deadly. This warning should lead us to a frequent and sincere examination of conscience, and to heartfelt repentance whenever we see the least hint of pride. Paul is not setting up an opposition, as if we must choose between charisms and love. It is not either–or, but both–and. His whole point is that God has given us charisms for the sake of love, and *exercising a charism must always be an act of love.*

James' Teaching on Healing

Paul's teaching on charisms is complemented by a brief passage on prayer for healing in the letter of James. James exhorts:

> Is any among you sick? Let him call for the el-
> ders of the Church, and let them pray over him,
> anointing him with oil in the name of the Lord;
> and the prayer of faith will save the sick man, and
> the Lord will raise him up; and if he has commit-
> ted sins, he will be forgiven.
>   Therefore confess your sins to one an-
> other, and pray for one another, that you may be
> healed. The prayer of a righteous man has great
> power in its effects. (Jas 5:14–16)

James describes two courses of action to take when a
member of the Church is sick. First, there is a rite of prayer
and anointing with oil carried out by the elders (presbyters)
of the Church. The Church recognizes this rite as the origin of
the sacrament of the Anointing of the Sick.[111] James declares
that the faith-filled prayer of the elders will "save" (*sōzō*) the
sick person and "the Lord will raise him up." Both these phras-
es have a twofold meaning, just as in the Gospels. On one level
they refer to a physical restoration to health. At the same time
they point to the fullness of salvation and bodily resurrection
that will occur on the last day. So we should not think that
the Anointing of the Sick is for spiritual strengthening only: at
its very origin it is a powerful instrument by which the Lord
brings bodily as well as spiritual healing.

The second part of the passage speaks of the ordinary
prayer of the faithful. James exhorts Christians first to confess
our sins to one another, reaffirming the principle that sin can
be an obstacle to healing. In the early Church this probably
referred to a public confession of sins,[112] whereas today we do
so privately in the Sacrament of Reconciliation. James then exhorts us to pray for one another that we may be healed. Here
the word for healing, *iaomai*, clearly refers to physical healing.
Seeking to arouse our faith that God really will hear our prayer
for one another, James goes on to give the example of Elijah:
"Elijah was a man of like nature with ourselves and he prayed

fervently that it might not rain, and for three years and six months it did not rain on the earth. Then he prayed again and the heaven gave rain, and the earth brought forth its fruit" (Jas 5:17–18). The point is that Elijah was not some heavenly being with supernatural powers, but a human being just like us. If we are living an upright life and have fervent faith like his, we too can see miracles as he did.

Church Teaching on the Charisms

Charisms have never ceased to be part of the life of the Church, yet for many centuries they were neglected in theology and preaching. At Vatican Council II, as St. John Paul II later pointed out, the Holy Spirit guided the Church into a rediscovery of the importance of charisms.[113] The Council strongly reaffirmed Paul's teaching that charisms are given by the Spirit to all the faithful and should be received gratefully:

> Allotting his gifts according as he wills (cf. 1 Cor 12:11), he [the Holy Spirit] also distributes special graces among the faithful of every rank. By these gifts he makes them fit and ready to undertake various tasks and offices for the renewal and building up of the Church, as it is written, 'the manifestation of the Spirit is given to everyone for profit' (1 Cor 12:7). Whether these charisms be very remarkable or more simple and widely diffused, they are to be received with thanksgiving and consolation since they are fitting and useful for the needs of the Church.[114]

The Council fathers also reiterated Paul's teaching that with God's gifts comes a responsibility to use them for the good of others.

From the acceptance of these charisms, including those which are more elementary, there arise
for each believer *the right and duty to use them* in
the Church and in the world for the good of men
and the building up of the Church, in the freedom of the Holy Spirit who "breathes where He
wills" (John 3:8). This should be done by the laity in communion with their brothers in Christ,
especially with their pastors who must make a
judgment about the true nature and proper use
of these gifts, not to extinguish the Spirit but to
test all things and hold for what is good (cf. 1
Thess 5:12, 19, 21).[115]

This statement is remarkable for its insistence that
charisms must be used in the freedom of the Holy Spirit. The
gifts are by definition spontaneous manifestations of the Holy
Spirit. The Spirit is the initiator; we follow. To attempt to control the gifts or force them into a preexisting structure is to
stifle them. Cardinal Ratzinger expressed this admonition
even more strongly:

The bishops ... must not turn their own pastoral
plans into the criterion of what the Holy Spirit is
allowed to do: an obsession with planning could
render the Churches impervious to the action of
the Holy Spirit, to the power of God by which
they live. Not everything should be fitted into the
straightjacket of a single uniform organization;
what is needed is less organization and more
Spirit![116]

The Council fathers taught, again following Paul, that
charisms must never be used independently. No one is the
owner of his or her charism; "no charism dispenses a person
from reference and submission to the Pastors of the Church."[117]

At the same time, bishops and all those who have authority to oversee the exercise of charisms must themselves rely on the Holy Spirit. They are not masters of the charisms. Their role is not to subordinate them to human plans, but to order them to the good of the Church and its mission.

St. John Paul II both promoted the use of charisms and used them himself. According to many testimonies, he had a charism of healing and often prayed over people, sometimes with remarkable results.[118] My friends the Foleys discovered that in an unexpected way. Dolly Foley recounts:

> Dan and I always wanted a large family. Our daughter Louise arrived just after our first anniversary. After that we had a miscarriage, and then nothing. The years went by. Louise graduated from college and was working on Capitol Hill. I told Dan, "If we have another child I'm going to call her Sarah Elizabeth, the child of our old age."
>
> Then we went to Rome for a conference, which included an audience with Pope John Paul II. We had very good seats, so the pope came down and talked to all of us. He greeted me, then moved on down the line. But then he came back, I don't know why, and placed his hand on my head for a moment. Later everyone said to me, "What did you ask him for? Why did he pray over you?" I said I had no idea.
>
> The very next year our daughter Sarah Elizabeth came along, twenty-four years after her sister.

What If You Don't Have the Charism?

Those who have a charism of healing will see an unusual number of remarkable healings when they pray with people. Yet you do not have to have the charism of healing to pray and see healings. Jesus said, "I tell you, ask, and it will be given you; seek, and you will find; knock, and it will be opened to you" (Luke 11:9). Ask for a greater release of the Holy Spirit in your life, step out in faith to pray for healing wherever it is needed, and God will delight in answering your prayer.

One of my students, Tony DiMaria, a parish evangelization coordinator, stepped out in faith at a meeting of his men's group one Saturday morning. Each of the men had mentioned their prayer requests, and Tony was leading the group in prayer. A newcomer, Dan, asked for prayers for his son who had been suffering from severe headaches for five weeks. The doctors could not determine the cause, and he was being tested at the hospital for blood vessel blockages. Tony recounts:

> Hearing Dan's concerned tone, my sense was immediate that we needed to pray over Dan's son even though he was not present. I thought of the scripture story of the Roman centurion (Matt 8:5–13). I said to the men, "Let's pray over Dan for his son. We all know that we pray during the liturgy, 'Lord, I am not worthy that you should enter under my roof, but only say the word,' which expresses the great faith of the Roman centurion that his servant did not need to be physically present for our Lord to heal him." Wayne, our other leader, then asked our men to extend their hands in prayer over Dan, and he and I laid hands on him.
>
> I stumbled through the prayer, struggling to find words to express our desire for the Holy Spirit's healing work for Dan's son. When I had completed the prayer I thought to myself, "Wow, that ruined a great spiritual moment with the men." I also thought, "I should have laid hands on his head, not on his shoulder as I did." But then I

thought, "Well, God doesn't need our eloquence to evidence his work. Here you go, Lord, do with it as you will."

A few days later I spoke with Dan, who in a tone of amazement and thankfulness said, "My son's severe headaches are gone. He was healed the same day of your prayer." His pain was ninety percent gone on the day we prayed. The remainder was gone in a few days, and he has been pain-free since then. Besides enlivening Dan's faith, his son was profoundly touched by how his dad showed his love through this prayer for him.

Dan then shared with Tony that he used to be Catholic and now felt that God was calling him back to the Catholic Church. Tony's simple act of faith had opened the door to both a physical and a spiritual healing.

CHAPTER NINE

Redemptive Suffering

*I rejoice in my sufferings for your sake, and in my flesh
I complete what is lacking in Christ's afflictions
for the sake of his body, that is, the Church.*

— Colossians 1:24

Some people call her the Mother Teresa of Mexico. Madre
Inés Valdivia González is in her late eighties but still runs an
orphanage for children with mental and physical disabilities,
Casa Hogar La Divina Providencia, near Mexico City. Despite
the poverty and suffering within its walls, the Casa is a place
of joy, laughter and peace. Among the many miracles that have
taken place there is the following, which Madre Inés recounted
to a missionary friend of mine who often visits the orphanage.

A man visited the Casa who had been diagnosed with
terminal cancer. He shared with Madre that since he did not
have much time left on earth, he realized he had better get
right with God. He decided to visit the orphanage as a way
of doing a good deed. She gave him a tour of the facility, including the upper floor where the most severely handicapped
children live. Madre Inés considers these her most precious
charges, believing that their souls are already in some way in
God's presence. Most of them simply lie on cots, drooling, in-
capable of movement or speech.

As the visitor walked through the room, the limp hand of
one boy brushed against him, so he sat down and held the boy's
hand for a few minutes as the child gazed intently into his eyes.

He felt good reaching out to this profoundly disadvantaged person. After a few minutes he smiled and walked on.

The next day he woke up feeling better than he had in some time. The next day he felt even better, and the next day better still. He went back to his doctor, and after some tests was informed that his body was completely cancer-free. When he called Madre Inés to share the good news, she told him that shortly after his visit, the boy whose hand he had held had passed away.

Grace Overflowing

This story illustrates the profound spiritual interconnection that exists among the members of the body of Christ. Did that handicapped boy in some mysterious way offer his life for the healing of the man who visited him? It is impossible to know for sure, but Catholic tradition has always recognized that the suffering of one member, lovingly offered up in Christ, can be a source of great grace for others. Because of our union with Christ, we are united with one another, and grace overflows from one to another.

Suffering therefore has inestimable value for those who are in Christ. But how does our appreciation for the value of suffering accord with prayer for healing? If suffering has great value, why should we ever pray for healing? Is it not better to embrace sickness for the good of ourselves and others? To answer these questions we must look at what Scripture teaches about suffering and its relationship to healing.

The Christian understanding of the value of suffering is rooted in the words of Jesus: "Whoever does not take up his cross and follow me is not worthy of me" (Matt 10:38; 16:24). To be a Christian is to walk in the footsteps of the suffering Son of Man, to accompany him on the way of the cross. Suffering is an inevitable part of every human life, but God uses it to purify and perfect his children. The letter to the Hebrews affirms that even Jesus, "Son though he was ... learned obedience from what he suffered" (5:8). Of course Jesus was never disobedient. Yet obedience, like all virtue, comes to perfection only by being tested in difficult circumstances. Like a coal that is crushed under enormous pressure until it becomes a diamond, his human nature, crushed under his passion, was brought to an infinite perfection of love and obedience to God. For a Christian, all the more is suffering needed for our growth to maturity as sons and daughters of God. "The Lord disciplines him whom he loves, and chastises every son whom he receives" (Heb 12:6). Suffering humbles us and softens our rough edges. It is God's chisel to shape the rough-hewn rock that we are into the magnificent statue he has created us to be.

Even more, suffering is an invitation to share in Christ's passion. Paul understood this deeply. He did not just endure afflictions but positively desired them: "For his sake I have suffered the loss of all things, and count them as refuse, in order that I may gain Christ and be found in him ... that I may know him and the power of his resurrection, and may share his sufferings, becoming like him in his death" (Phil 3:8–10). Paul experienced that suffering had a unique capacity to soften his heart and configure him to the self-giving love of Jesus. Suffering therefore prepares us for the glory that will one day be ours: we are "heirs of God and fellow heirs with Christ, provided we suffer with him in order that we may also be glorified with him" (Rom 8:17).[119]

Yet another gift is that when our suffering is offered in union with Christ, it becomes a means of grace for others. Paul tells the Corinthians, "If we are afflicted, it is for your comfort and salvation; and if we are comforted, it is for your comfort" (2 Cor 1:6). Paul means more than that he is willing to endure the hardships of an itinerant apostolic life to bring them the gospel. His sufferings actually become a conduit of saving grace for them (2 Cor 4:10–12). In his letter to the Colossians he develops this insight further: "I rejoice in my sufferings for your sake, and in my flesh I complete what is lacking in Christ's afflictions for the sake of his body, that is, the Church" (Col 1:24). This is a startling claim! How can anything be lacking in Christ's afflictions? As St. John Paul II noted, Paul does not mean that Christ's redemption is incomplete itself. Christ's once-for-all sacrifice is all-sufficient to redeem the whole world (Heb 10:10). Yet in the Lord's overflowing generosity, he gives us the privilege of participating in his work of redemption. "Those who share in the sufferings of Christ preserve in their own sufferings a very special *particle of the infinite treasure* of the world's Redemption, and can share this treasure with others."[120]

Two Kinds of Suffering

There is a distinction among biblical passages about suffering that often goes unnoticed today. When Jesus exhorts his disciples to expect suffering and to rejoice in it, he is referring to *the trials associated with persecution for the sake of the gospel.*[121] They are what might be called apostolic sufferings — the persecution, mockery, and hardships that often go with being a Christian and sharing the gospel with others. For example, Jesus said, "Blessed are you when men hate you, and when they exclude you and revile you, and cast out your name as evil, on account of the Son of man! Rejoice in that day, and leap for joy, for behold, your reward is great in heaven" (Luke 6:22–23). When, in contrast, Jesus encounters physical or emotional *sickness*, he invariably responds with healing. He confronts sickness as an evil to be overcome rather than a good to be embraced.

Likewise when Paul speaks about embracing his afflictions, they are those resulting from apostolic labors and persecution — imprisonment, beatings, stoning, shipwreck, danger, sleepless nights, hunger and thirst, exposure, anxiety for the churches.[122] Catholic tradition has always regarded it as legitimate to extend the theology of redemptive suffering to every kind of suffering, including sickness. However, it does not follow that our response to sickness should be the same as our response to apostolic suffering, as will be seen below.

Don't Waste Your Pain

My friend Robin Beck has experienced the grace of redemptive suffering in a powerful way. She suffers from scoliosis, arthritis, osteoporosis, and several other painful conditions. When she became a Catholic just a few years ago, she was thrilled to learn that her afflictions could be used to empower her prayer for others. She does not pray for healing for herself because she feels called to use her sufferings as weapons in her arsenal as she intercedes for grace and mercy for others. She uses her pain to maximum effect. She says things like, "My knee has been sore all week. That's for you. My hip is for my cousin's daughter who is going through a divorce." She writes half-jokingly:

> One of the messages I have received from the Lord in the midst of my suffering is, "Don't waste your pain!" Translated: Offer it all up! A hospital stay, especially when surgery is involved, is a great time to plan on praying for everyone you know. When the nurse walks in your room holding a hypo that's bigger than a knitting needle one would use for a hippopotamus, pick a name from your prayer list and offer it up for them. After the ninetieth time of being poked (and when all your veins have collapsed), you'll be in such a state of grace you won't care what they've come to jab you with. If you stay focused on using the gift of pain for others you're hospital stay will become a holy pilgrimage where you do the Spirit's

bidding in the lives of others. Never doubt for
one minute how much that will please the Father.

How much wasted suffering there is in the world today! How many people are lying in hospitals or nursing homes
simply enduring their pain and loneliness, or even letting bitterness fester. If only they knew how much potential their suffering has for empowering the Church's mission to bring the
light of Christ into the world. Often it is because no one has
told them; no one has called upon their intercessory muscle.
If they lovingly offer their sufferings in union with Christ, especially if they offer it for specific intentions, their seemingly
useless lives will actually be bearing abundant fruit. As one
priest I know says, "Their lives are not a waste, they are the
Marine Corps of the Church!"

Any individual or parish that is initiating a ministry or
evangelistic endeavor would do well to look for such longsuf-
fering people and enlist their intercessory help, supporting
them in turn with prayer and following up with regular reports on how their prayers are being answered.

Human Physicians and the Divine Physician

The enormous intercessory potential of suffering makes the
question even more acute: why should we pray for healing at
all, when suffering can be so fruitful?

First, there is an important distinction: Christian tradition has never regarded suffering as good in itself. Rather,
suffering, pain, sickness and death are evils that came into the
world because of sin.[123] They were not God's original intention for the sons and daughters he created in his image. They
came into the world not by God's will but as a result of *rebellion against* God's will. But the amazing good news proclaimed
in the gospel is that God is able to bring good even out of evil.
"We know that all things work for good for those who love

God, who are called according to his purpose" (Rom 8:28). The apex of this divine power is manifested in the cross, where the unimaginable evil and pain inflicted on God's beloved Son, embraced by him in love, became the source of salvation for the whole world.

The recognition that suffering is an objective evil is the basis for all human efforts to alleviate it. Throughout Scripture God instructs his people again and again to relieve suffering: "share your bread with the hungry, and bring the homeless poor into your house; when you see the naked, cover him;... satisfy the desire of the afflicted" (Isa 58:6–10); visit the sick and imprisoned (Matt 25:31–46). Catholics through history have taken this instruction very seriously, building an immense array of hospitals, medical clinics, hospices, and other ministries with the express purpose of healing the sick insofar as possible and lessening every form of suffering.

Why then, it must be asked, would we do so much on a natural level to heal sickness, and yet hesitate to seek supernatural healing? We understand that there is no contradiction between the redemptive value of suffering and our intense human efforts to bring healing. Why would we think there is a contradiction between the redemptive value of suffering and asking *God* for healing? What would you think of a doctor who, upon diagnosing a patient with cancer, says to him, "Sorry, I'm not going to treat you because it's better that you simply accept this cross in your life. Offer it up." He'd be fired on the spot![124] Why then would any disciple of Jesus — one who has access to unlimited divine grace and power — upon hearing that someone is ill, respond in like manner?

Likewise, we should examine our response when confronted with illness in our own bodies. Ironically, Catholics faced with illness usually have no hesitation in seeking medical treatment, yet many are reluctant to ask God for healing. They assume God must want them to suffer. They go to the doctor, but not to the divine Physician. This reluctance is often based on a distorted view of God, as the God eager to mete out the punishment we deserve. In reality he is the God who is rich in mercy, who delights to lavish on us the grace we don't deserve.

Our first response to sickness, then, should be to do battle against it through faith and prayer. Jesus' response to illness and infirmity in the Gospels is a challenge to our attitudes of passivity. In the sick who besieged him he saw children of God who were bound up and blocked from the fullness of life God had for them. He "released" them, "opened" their eyes or ears or mouth, and "rebuked" sickness.[125] After raising Lazarus from the dead he called his disciples in turn to "unbind" one who had been bound by the cords of death (John 11:44).

Catholic theology is often a matter of both–and rather than either–or. Is Jesus Christ fully God or fully man? Both (cf. Phil 2:6–8). Is our faith based on Scripture or Tradition? Both (cf. 2 Thess 2:15). Are we justified by faith or works? Both (cf. Gal 2:15; Jas 2:24). Should we embrace our suffering in love, or pray for healing with expectant faith? *Both!* (cf. 1 Pet 4:13; Jas 5:16).

When to Desist

Then is there ever a time to stop praying for healing? How do we discern when that is? There is no hard and fast rule that can cover every instance. Praying for healing is letting the Holy Spirit lead the dance, not following a rule book. But there are a couple of simple principles that may be helpful. First, the Lord will often give an interior sense that it is time to change the prayer. Especially when praying for people who have lived a full span of life, the grace they may need is to be ready to meet the Lord. After all, the human mortality rate is one hundred percent. Second, we can pray differently when a sick or disabled person comes to a profound peace and joy in the midst of their suffering, no longer desiring healing because they see that the Lord is bringing great fruit out of their affliction. Their suffering has become a priestly offering in accord with Paul's exhortation: "present your bodies as a living sacrifice, holy and acceptable to God, which is your spiritual worship" (Rom 12:1).

Let us never hesitate to ask for the help of the divine Physician, any more than we should hesitate to go to earthly physicians. "Heal me, O LORD, and I shall be healed; save me, and I shall be saved; for you are my praise" (Jer 17:14).

Dr. Bob Sawyer, M.D., is a retired ear, nose, and throat specialist in Baltimore. He had been used by God to heal on a natural level for decades, but he did not realize the supernatural power that was also available to him in Christ. A few years ago, he began praying for more grace to overflow in his life. He recounts:

> I'd been asking the Lord to make his presence in me palpable to the people around me, that even when I step on an elevator they would somehow sense God. Not that they would be drawn to me, but that they would simply become more aware of God. One morning the chief nurse in surgery came and said, "There's a nurse friend of mine who has a brain tumor. Would you mind praying with her?" I asked if this other nurse knew me. "No, but she wants you to pray with her." I said of course I'd be willing. An hour later the woman came up to my office. She explained that the other day she had stepped on the elevator and looked at me, and something on my face had convinced her I was the one to pray with her.
>
> She was scheduled the next morning to have the definitive test to determine if her brain tumor was cancerous. This was a woman who hadn't gone to church in years, but she was desperate. She had two little kids and didn't want

to die. I said, "Okay, I'll be happy to pray with you." But I had zero faith that anything would happen. First I led her in a prayer to rededicate herself to the Lord, then a prayer to be baptized in the Holy Spirit. Then I prayed with her for healing. She thanked me and left.

The next day she went for the tests, and there was no sign of any tumor whatsoever.

A year later I was standing in front of an elevator as she stepped off. I asked, "How are things going?" She said, "It's amazing. Everything has changed. I now witness to my patients about what Jesus has done in my life and how he can change their lives." She and her kids were going to church on a regular basis.

Dr. Bob now often leads healing services in inner city parishes, with the full support of his archdiocese, and sees remarkable healings on a regular basis.

CHAPTER TEN

Saints and Sacraments

*They anointed with oil many that were sick
and healed them.*

— Mark 6:13

Fr. Francis Martin was serving as associate pastor at St. Paul's Parish in Damascus, Maryland. When he heard that a parishioner had just been diagnosed with a brain tumor larger than a golf ball, Fr. Francis decided to give him the Anointing of the Sick at Sunday Mass, in the presence of the whole congregation. He saw it as a teaching moment. He recounts:

> It was day before the doctor was going to operate. After the homily I called Marty up to the front, and I said to everyone, "Look, this is a sacrament. It always works. It may not produce the result we're looking for. But this is a sacrament, and the Lord is going to act. So watch."
>
> After I gave him the sacrament and prayed over him, I had a profound inner sense that the Lord had healed him. I said to Marty, "You might just ask the doctor to double check before he opens up your skull, because I think the Lord has done something. See if he can do one more test."
>
> The next morning, the doctor reluctantly agreed to do another test. There was no tumor. The surgery was canceled.

The next Sunday I told everybody and said, "Now, that was a sign for all of us: Are we going to listen to the word of God? The Lord is saying, "I am powerful enough to do anything in your lives. But I do expect obedience."

The sacraments are particularly efficacious ways in which Christ the divine Physician continues his work of healing through the Church. The *Catechism* teaches that just as Jesus touched and healed the sick during his earthly ministry, "so in the sacraments Christ continues to 'touch' us in order to heal us."[126] The Church "believes in the life-giving presence of Christ, the physician of souls and bodies. This presence is particularly active through the sacraments, and in an altogether special way through the Eucharist, the bread that gives eternal life and that St. Paul suggests is connected with bodily health."[127]

The sacraments are grounded in the recognition that the body and matter are part of the goodness of creation and can be used by God as vehicles of his grace. Scripture teaches this sacramental understanding of the world. Jesus sometimes healed people by his mere word, but at other times he used a physical means: the laying on of hands or saliva or clay.[128] Even the fringe of his garment could be a vehicle of his healing power (Matt 9:20–22). In Acts, handkerchiefs or aprons that Paul had touched were used to heal (Acts 19:12). In the Old Testament, a dead man was raised up by touching the bones of the prophet Elisha (2 Kgs 13:21).

God's use of matter to heal scandalizes some who would prefer that God act on a purely spiritual plane, or who think the use of physical objects for healing is a form of superstition. Yet Catholic teaching has always rejected an artificial division between the soul and body, as if God is concerned only with the soul. Tertullian, a third-century Father, wrote eloquently about how it is through our flesh that Christ mediates his grace:

The flesh is the hinge of salvation.... The flesh is
washed so that the soul may be made clean. The
flesh is anointed so that the soul may be conse-
crated. The flesh is signed so that the soul may
be protected. The flesh is overshadowed by the
laying on of hands so that the soul may be illu-
mined by the Spirit. The flesh feeds on the body
and blood of Christ so that the soul too may be
filled with God. [Flesh and spirit] cannot, then,
be separated in their reward, when they are united in their works.[129]

The healing power of the sacraments is manifested in a
special way in the two sacraments of healing, Reconciliation
and the Anointing of the Sick.[130] But in a sense all the sacraments can be understood as sacraments of healing, since all
are efficacious for the healing of fallen human nature.[131] It is
preeminently in the Eucharist, the heart of Christian life, in
which Christ's total gift of himself on the cross is made present and available to us, that we experience his healing power.
St. Ignatius called the Eucharist the "medicine of immortality."[132] So our response at Mass immediately before receiving
Holy Communion is an act of faith in Christ's healing: "Lord, I
am not worthy that you should enter under my roof, but only
say the word and my soul will be healed."[133] In the Byzantine
Catholic liturgy, the prayer before Communion more explicitly includes physical healing: "May the communion of Thy
holy Mysteries be neither to my judgment, nor to my condemnation, O Lord, but to the healing of soul and body."[134]

The Anointing of the Sick

Over time the Anointing of the Sick evolved in a way that
partly mirrored a shift in the understanding of healing. As the
Catechism observes, "Over the centuries the Anointing of the

Sick was conferred more and more exclusively on those at the point of death. Because of this it received the name 'Extreme Unction.'"[135] Although the sacramental rite never ceased to include prayers for healing, the emphasis changed to an almost exclusive focus on preparation for a holy death. People actually dreaded the appearance of a priest to administer this sacrament, because it was seen as a herald of death!

Vatican Council II called for a revision of the rite to restore its original character as a sacrament of healing, both by reinstating its former name and by directing that it is for all the seriously ill, not only those in danger of death.[136] The revision, completed in 1974, changed the essential form of the sacrament to more strongly emphasize healing.[137] The prayer for blessing the oil to be used in the sacrament explicitly mentions physical healing: "May your blessing come upon all who are anointed with this oil, that they may be freed from pain and illness and made well again in body, mind, and soul." Many priests attest to having witnessed miraculous healings through this sacrament, like the disappearance of the brain tumor recounted above. Yet unfortunately, a low expectation of physical healing is still common.

Healing through the Intercession
of the Saints

Scripture teaches that during our earthly journey we are "surrounded by a great cloud of witnesses," the saints who have gone before us and are now cheering us on toward the finish line (Heb 12:1). Because of our union with Christ, we are united with all those who are in him, in heaven and purgatory as well as on earth.[138] The saints in heaven, more closely united to Christ than we can imagine, intercede for us constantly, and the Lord often uses their prayers to pour out grace and healing on earth.

One of the most remarkable healings that has come down to us from the early Church took place through the intercession of St. Stephen the Martyr. It occurred at St. Augustine's cathedral at Hippo in North Africa. Augustine attests that this miracle was so striking that no resident of the city was unaware of it or could possibly forget it. It involved a brother and sister named Paulus and Palladia, who were afflicted with constant and severe tremors throughout their bodies. They had wandered far and wide, and eventually found themselves in Hippo. Augustine reports what happened:

> Now it was about fifteen days before Easter when they came, and they came daily to church, and especially to the relics of the most glorious Stephen, praying that God might now be appeased, and restore their former health.[139] There, and wherever they went, they attracted the attention of everyone....
>
> Easter arrived, and on the Lord's day in the morning, when there was a large crowd present and the young man was holding the bars of the holy place where the relics were, praying, suddenly he fell down and lay precisely as if asleep, but not trembling as he used to do even in sleep. All present were astonished. Some were alarmed, some were moved with pity. While some were in favor of lifting him up, others prevented them, and said they should rather wait and see what would happen. And behold! he rose up and trembled no more, for he was healed, and stood quite well, looking at those who were looking at him.

Paulus' suddenly falling down and lying as if asleep was probably what is today called "resting in the Spirit." This is a common phenomenon in settings where there is healing prayer ministry, or where people are prayed over for an outpouring of the Holy Spirit. It is a human response to the overwhelming presence and power of the Holy Spirit. Very often, the Lord uses this temporary suspension of faculties to do a profound work of healing, just as a heart surgeon works best while his patient is under anesthesia.

Augustine continues:

> Who then refrained from praising God? The whole church was filled with the voices of those who were shouting and congratulating him. Then they came running to me, where I was sitting ready to come into the church. One after another they throng in, the last comer telling me as news what the first had told me already. And while I rejoiced and inwardly gave thanks to God, the young man himself enters with a number of others, falls at my knees, and is raised up to receive my kiss. We go in to the congregation: the church was full, and ringing with shouts of joy, "Thanks be to God! Praised be God!" everyone joining and shouting on all sides, "I have healed the people," and then with still louder voice shouting again.

Augustine shows not the slightest inclination to calm the excited emotions of his congregation or to stop their loud shouting. He recognizes that exuberant praise is the right response to a mighty work of God. The people are thrilled that God has had mercy on this man whom they had pitied and prayed for. As the psalm proclaims, "It is good to give thanks to the LORD, to sing praise to your name, Most High.... For you make me jubilant, LORD, by your deeds; at the works of your hands I shout for joy" (Ps 92:2–5).

> When silence was at last obtained, the customary readings of the divine Scriptures were read. And when I came to my sermon, I made a few

remarks suitable to the occasion and the happy and joyful feeling, not wanting them to listen to me but rather to consider the eloquence of God in this divine work. The man dined with us and gave us a careful account of his family's calamity. Accordingly, on the following day, after delivering my sermon, I promised that I would read his narrative to the people.

Augustine's response to this totally unexpected situation is a model of pastoral wisdom. He recognized that this miracle was a divine visitation. He therefore let the Holy Spirit run the show. He did not attempt to get everything under control and go on as usual as if nothing out of the ordinary had happened. Brilliant orator though he was, he put aside his prepared homily and simply made a few spontaneous remarks so as not to deflect attention from the eloquence of God himself in this mighty deed.

Recognizing that testimonies have a unique power to stir up faith, Augustine also saw to it that at Mass the whole congregation heard a testimony of this healing in Paulus' own words.

And when I did so, the third day after Easter Sunday, I made the brother and sister both stand on the steps of the raised place from which I used to speak, and while they stood there their account was read. The whole congregation, men and women alike, saw the one standing without any unnatural movement, the other trembling in all her limbs.... In him they saw reason for congratulation, in her they saw subject for prayer.

Meanwhile, their account being finished, I instructed them to withdraw from the gaze of the people. I had begun to discuss the whole matter somewhat more carefully, when lo!

as I was proceeding, other voices are heard
from the tomb of the martyr, shouting new
congratulations. My audience turned round, and
began to run to the tomb. The young woman had
gone to pray at the holy relics, and no sooner had
she touched the bars than she, in the same way
as her brother, collapsed as if falling asleep, and
rose up cured. While we were asking what had
happened, and what occasioned this noise of joy,
they came into the basilica, leading her from the
martyr's tomb in perfect health.

Then indeed, such a shout of wonder
rose from men and women together, that the ex-
clamations and tears seemed they would never
come to an end. She was led to the place where
she had a little earlier stood trembling. They now
rejoiced that she was like her brother, and since
they had not yet uttered their prayers in her be-
half, they perceived that their intention of doing
so had been quickly heard. They shouted God's
praises without words, but with such a noise that
our ears could scarcely bear it. What was there in
the hearts of these exultant people but the faith of
Christ, for which Stephen had shed his blood?[140]

It is a profoundly moving scene. Augustine has barely
begun the difficult task of explaining with careful theological
nuance why some people get healed and some do not, when
God spares him the trouble. His sermon is interrupted with
new shouts of elation, quickly spreading to the whole congregation as they realize what has happened: God has once again
displayed his awesome power. Augustine brings Palladia up to
the front so everyone can see her, now in perfect health like
her brother. There is such solidarity among the members of
the church that they all exult as if they themselves had been
healed. "If one member suffers, all suffer together; if one

member is honored, all rejoice together" (1 Cor 12:26). Tears flow freely. Praise raises the roof. People exalt God aloud yet "without words" — that is, using the gift of tongues.[141] It is a scene of holy chaos. Surely no one who participated in it could ever forget this display of the mercy of God.

Brought to Jesus by Mary

God in his generosity has given his children sacraments, saints, and an inexhaustible variety of ways in which to access his healing power. Sometimes a healing occurs through a combination of different avenues of grace.

Sarah Singer's healing did not come quickly, but when it did it involved a both a saint (the greatest saint) and two sacraments.

Sarah's migraines began when she was twelve years old. Each one would last for three weeks, followed by a week off, then another for three weeks. That was only the beginning.

In her teens Sarah started developing severe pain in her jaw. Visits to the dentist resulted only in his assurance that there was nothing wrong. The pain gradually spread to her neck, then her shoulders and back, then throughout her body. Over the years, three bouts of shingles left her in constant pain in both hips. It eventually came to the point where Sarah thought she would lose her mind. She would go to bed in pain and wake up in more pain. She remembers,

> I started to have what I called "screaming head-aches" — kind of beyond the beyond of mi-graines. Later they analyzed it as trigeminal neu-ralgia. I had teeth pulled out because I couldn't take the pain.
>
> It took years for the doctors to diagnose fibromyalgia and begin to treat it, but even then nothing helped. I can't even tell you how many

pills I have tried. Later I couldn't drive. I lost the ability to concentrate. I had to retire from my job with disability. I remember saying to my husband, "The only thing that's ahead of me is falling apart." I became fairly bedridden. My pain level was around eleven [out of ten]. I had to wear two pairs of sunglasses and put stuff in my ears so noise wouldn't bother me.

I would talk to the Lord in prayer, and at one point I thought he said, "I want you to come to me through Mary." It was a new idea that I didn't quite feel comfortable with. But I began to pray and journal with Mary a little bit. She had patience and a sense of humor, and in small ways I started to talk to her.

One day at Mass we had the reading about the man at the pool who had been sick for 38 years, and he needed somebody to carry him to the water. I felt like Jesus was saying, "I want Mary to carry you to me." After Mass Fr. Francis gave me the Anointing of the Sick. A few weeks later, at the beginning of May, I suddenly became aware that there was no pain in my head. It was amazing. Then the next day pain was dropping out of my neck, and the next day out of my back, and then out of my hips. I was becoming pain free. The next day it dropped out of my legs, then my feet. And the last place it dropped out of was my heels. All of a sudden I had no pain in my body. It was a miracle.

That was about seven years ago and I've been well ever since.

CHAPTER ELEVEN

Healing of the Heart

He heals the brokenhearted and
binds up their wounds.
— Psalm 147:3

There was a lot of pain in Robin Beck's life (the same Robin mentioned in chapter 9). Both her parents had been alcoholics. Although her father had stopped drinking before she was born, he had a volatile temper and was sometimes physically abusive toward his wife and kids. Her mother was depressed and detached, showing little affection. Because her dad was the more involved parent, Robin was closer to him and identified with him. She grew up deeply confused, believing that the people who really loved you might kill you one day.

By the time she was in high school Robin was also confused about her gender identity. Since she had seen her mother abused, weak and helpless, she wanted nothing to do with being a woman. For a period of time a male teacher and his wife welcomed Robin into their family, but when their welcome wore out, Robin experienced a deep sense of rejection. Her heart became completely closed off to men.

As a young adult Robin encountered the love of Christ and gave her life to him. But the brokenness in her heart had not been healed. Shortly thereafter, she had her first lesbian experience. "From this point on," she says, "I slid into the abyss."

> I was in one relationship after another, most of
> them lasting no longer than eighteen months.
> I tried to convince myself God was okay with

my behavior. I tried to reinterpret Scripture that identified it as sinful. Living this lie took a toll on me. I attempted suicide several times and had an eating disorder for years. I was always drawn to churches where the Truth was being proclaimed, but when the "gay issue" came up, that was my cue to exit. Churches that accepted homosexual behavior were void of the power of the gospel because they ignored the cross, never mentioned sin, and Jesus was just a nice guy who let us all get away with doing whatever we wanted to do. I never lasted very long at those churches.

One day a Catholic friend asked Robin if she'd like to join her for Mass on Ash Wednesday and "do ashes." Robin had never been to a Mass. Having been raised a Baptist, she had been taught that Catholics worshiped statues, prayed to the dead, and believed all kinds of false doctrines. But the idea of getting ashes intrigued her, so she came.

At Mass, Robin sat startled and confused as her stereotypes melted before her eyes. The whole liturgy was saturated with Scripture. The congregation sang fervently and participated with reverence. The presence of God was palpable. As people lined up to receive ashes, then holy Communion, Robin sat with tears streaming down her face. Her friend took advantage of the situation to ask if she'd like to come again on Sunday. "Yes, by all means!" She came that Sunday, and the next, and the next.

Robin knew her lifestyle was not in accord with God's will. But what she did not realize at the time was that that visit to Mass was the beginning of a long healing journey.

God harpooned my heart that afternoon at Mass. Seven months later, when my latest relationship fell apart, I got down on my knees and surrendered my messed-up life to Jesus. I repented of homosexual sin, walked away from a life of destruction and never looked back.

I signed up for an RCIA class and began to radically change my life. I got rid of my TV, of DVDs and music that triggered memories of gay culture, and began to listen to Christian radio from morning till night. I seriously read the Bible, asking the Lord to help me see Truth. God was so faithful.

From the first day I walked away from the homosexual lifestyle, I was committed to chastity. But I knew I was pretty messed up on the inside and had no clue to heal my life. That's when Jesus took over and began to direct my steps.

I received prayer ministry from a couple at another parish, who prayed using the Unbound model.[142] Through that prayer I was released from old bondages caused by bitterness, resentments and an unforgiving heart. I was deeply touched by the love of Jesus pouring through the man who was my spiritual guide that afternoon. My heart was rebirthed that day as far as men went.

I also began to meet with a small group of women on Saturday mornings. We shared our pain, old wounds, relationships that were broken, and then we prayed for each other with laying on of hands and prophetic words. God used this group to teach me how to have healthy relationships with other women.

At charismatic prayer meetings I experienced special encounters with Jesus, especially when we could go up before the tabernacle and lie on our faces underneath the cross.

I learned to draw on the power of the sacraments. Before becoming Catholic at the Easter Vigil, I went to the Sacrament of Reconciliation to confess my sexual sin. Afterward I ran to Mass often to receive the Eucharist and God's healing mercy. I later received the Anointing of the Sick and specifically asked Jesus to heal my damaged soul from the effects of homosexual behavior.

Now, five years later, I am free of same-sex attractions. I love being a woman and embrace my femininity.[143]

Through the sacraments, healing prayer ministry, and the faithful love of brothers and sisters in Christ, over a long period of time the Lord has healed layer upon layer of hurt in Robin's heart. Jesus the great Physician is an expert at healing the human heart, wounded and bruised by the traumas of life, by the sins committed against us, and by our own sins and coping mechanisms.

Jesus at the Well

The story of Jesus' encounter with the Samaritan woman in John 4 reveals much about how Jesus heals inner wounds. The setting of the story, Jacob's well, provides an initial clue to its meaning. In a biblical context a well is a place where, in a seemingly chance encounter, bridegroom meets bride. The patriarch Jacob found his beloved bride at a well, as did Isaac and Moses (Gen 24; 29; Exod 2:15–21). This scriptural background prepares us to see the meeting at the well as more than a simple conversation. It is a divine romance, the Lord wooing the heart of one he loves, who had wandered far away from him.

The woman comes to draw water at noon, the hottest time of day, the time when she is least likely to run into the other women of the village. Why? As the story unfolds we learn that she has not exactly been living an upright moral life. In fact her life has been a series of failed relationships. She has had five husbands and is now living with another man (John 4:18).[144] Evidently she feels ashamed and embarrassed about her history of rejection and sexual sin. Perhaps she is used to being hassled, ridiculed, gossiped about, or ostracized by her neighbors.

The way Jesus speaks to her is striking. As a Jewish man, he ignores the cultural taboos that would prevent him from speaking publicly to a Samaritan woman. Jesus addresses her not "from above," with a stern admonishment to reform her behavior, but "from beneath," as a beggar. He asks this woman who may have lost all confidence in her own goodness to do something for him: "Give me a drink." He neither moralizes, nor pities, nor judges her, but simply accepts her as she is. As the conversation progresses, Jesus offers her the gift of living water to quench her deepest thirst.

Without yet fully understanding, she asks for this living water. But Jesus makes an unexpected reply: "Go, call your husband, and come here" (John 4:16). Why this seeming digression? As the divine Physician, Jesus is probing the very area where she is wounded, revealing her futile pursuit of security and comfort through relationships with men. He is exposing the darkness in her heart, precisely so that he can heal it. As he does so, she is looking into his eyes and sees his absolute lack of condemnation. When the Lord brings to light our sin and woundedness, it is never to condemn, only to bring us to the repentance that leads to freedom.

At a deeper level, this woman's life story embodies the history of her people. After Samaria, or northern Israel, was conquered by the Assyrians in 722 B.C., five foreign peoples were resettled there, each with its god (2 Kgs 17:24–31).[145]

These false gods were worshiped with the title Baal, which means "husband." But through the prophets, God had promised that he would heal Israel's spiritual adultery. Against this biblical background the deeper significance of the encounter at the well comes to light: Jesus, the Word made flesh, is the divine bridegroom inviting this woman, and her whole nation, to leave their false gods and return to the Lord, their first and true husband, the only one who truly loves them.

At the end of the conversation her heart is deeply stirred as she begins to wonder just who it is who is standing before her: can this be the Messiah? Jesus answers, "It is I who speak to you," or literally, "*I am* who speak to you" (4:26), echoing the divine name revealed to Moses at the burning bush (Exod 3:14). Jesus is not only revealing his identity as the Messiah but hinting at his identity as the Lord God. It is an astounding self-revelation, one not yet given to anyone else in the Gospel, even his disciples. Why is it given to her, a woman who is a nobody in the eyes of society — seemingly the person least worthy? Simply because the Lord sees in her a heart that is thirsty and open to him.

At this dramatic revelation, the woman abandons her water jug — for she has now drunk of the living water — and goes home full of excitement, proclaiming the good news to all her townspeople (John 4:29–30). Those who knew her as a lonely outcast can see the unmistakable joy on her face, the transformation of a once broken and empty life. It is enough to make them want to come and meet Jesus for themselves, to drink of the living water that has now become a fountain within her.

This story illustrates that it is first and foremost an encounter with Jesus that heals the human heart. We are created for God, and only God can satisfy the thirst within. The primary goal of healing ministry, therefore, is always to bring a person into an encounter with Jesus. Jesus alone knows the person from within — all their hurts, their sins and failures, their disappointments, their buried dreams. Jesus alone is able to reach into the depths of the person's memory and bring wholeness and freedom. The role of the one praying is to create a space for that encounter and step aside, allowing the Lord to meet his beloved.

Why Have You Torn Your Clothes?

The Church is indeed a field hospital, and it follows that Christians are meant to be the medical personnel who are prepared, trained and equipped to bring comfort and healing to the wounded.

The Second Book of Kings recounts how the king of Syria wrote a letter to the king of Israel, saying that he was sending his military officer Naaman to be healed of leprosy. The king had heard a rumor, through Naaman's servant girl, that the God of Israel was a God who healed the sick. But when the king of Israel read the letter his response was to tear his robes. He assumed that the king of Syria was just looking for an excuse to pick a fight. What could he possibly do about an army officer with a deadly disease?

But when Elisha the prophet heard that the king of Israel had torn his clothes, he sent him a message: "Why have you torn your clothes? Let him come now to me, that he may know that there is a prophet in Israel" (2 Kgs 5:8). Elisha was chiding the king for his lack of faith. Is there not a God in Israel? Is he not the God of miracles? Does he not have a prophet who believes in him and will pray to him for healing with confident faith?

Elisha's message can serve as an examination of conscience for Christians today. When we encounter deeply wounded people, especially those interiorly wounded by the family breakdown and sexual disorder that is rampant in our culture, what is our response? Do we simply reiterate the Church's moral teachings and tell them in effect, "Good luck, do the best you can, and don't forget to go to confession"? Or do we believe in a God of power? Do we believe God is able to heal the human heart at the deepest level and restore people to wholeness? Do we provide ways for people to experience that healing through prayer ministry as well as the sacraments in an environment of expectant faith?

The ministry of inner healing is a neglected but essential tool for the New Evangelization. Every parish that is seeking to be completely mission-oriented, as Pope Francis has directed, should establish a healing ministry team that is available for those who need either physical healing or healing of the heart. The team should consist of parishioners who are spiritually mature, trustworthy, and well trained. An excellent Catholic resource for such training is Neal and Janet Lozano's Unbound Ministry.[146]

Demolishing Strongholds

There is another kind of healing that Jesus constantly carried out during his public ministry: deliverance from evil spirits.[147] He also commissioned his disciples to cast out demons, continuing his work of overthrowing the dominion of Satan and liberating those who were held captive.[148] The ministry of deliverance is closely related to healing and includes every effort to help people break free by the grace of Jesus Christ from all the deception and bondage of the evil one. Deliverance is distinct from major exorcism, which is a liturgical rite of the Church carried out only in cases of demonic possession (which are very rare), and which can only be done by a bishop or by a priest duly appointed by bishop.[149]

Deliverance ministry is an extension of the prayer that Jesus taught in the Our Father: "deliver us from evil." It recognizes the fact that evil spirits are able to get a foothold in our lives through our sin or through the wounds we have received from others. Even for those living a godly Christian life, there can be inner areas of bondage: fear, compulsion, a deep sense of rejection, or hidden sins that keep us from the freedom and fullness of life that is our inheritance in Christ. Deliverance prayer — exercising the authority we have in Christ to expel these evil spirits from our lives, and helping others do so — is part of the normal Christian life.[150]

I saw firsthand the effect of deliverance prayer one evening when I was with a mission team at a church in Brazil. A young woman whom I'll call Laura came up in the line to receive prayer. She looked like someone who had already been beaten down by life. Her shoulders were hunched over and her face grayish. Looking at her I estimated her age at around thirty. I was taken aback when she told me she was sixteen. I asked what she wanted prayer for, and she hesitantly said she was being troubled by demons. This is not uncommon to hear in Latin America, where religious syncretism and occult practices are common. So my young Portuguese interpreter and I began to pray over her.

After a few minutes, I sensed that there was some obstacle blocking the prayer. Since a major obstacle to healing is unforgiveness (Mark 11:25), I asked Laura if there was anyone she needed to forgive. After hesitating a moment, she confided that one of the pastors at her church had repeatedly molested her, beginning when she was eleven. I said, "I am so sorry to hear that. That was a very grave sin against you. It's important for you to know that forgiveness does not mean minimizing the sin. It is simply to leave it in the hands of God. God will judge that man. But you can let go of any resentment toward him, and be free." She agreed to forgive him, and I led her in a prayer of forgiveness.

Realizing that such a trauma can also lead to other kinds of spiritual bondage, I explained to Laura that she could take authority over any other ways the evil one may have gotten a foothold in her life. I led her in a series of simple prayers: "In the name of Jesus, I renounce shame. In the name of Jesus,

I renounce fear. In the name of Jesus, I renounce guilt." When I mentioned guilt, Laura broke in: "I think it was my fault." I assured her that it was not, that at her young age she could not be responsible. I knew that my words alone could not convince her. Only the Lord could free her from that lie.

As we continued to pray, I invited Laura to say, "In the name of Jesus, I renounce idolatry." Up to this point she had unhesitatingly repeated the prayers, but when she tried to say "In the name of Jesus, I renounce idolatry," suddenly her mouth clamped shut. She tried several times but could not get the word out. I knew this was a sign of demonic influence compromising her freedom in this area.

At this point the interpreter, who was new to healing prayer, tried to be helpful. He got in her face and said loudly in Portuguese, "Repeat! I renounce i-do-la-try. Come on. *I renounce i* — " I gently stopped him and explained that we had to address her free will, not her speech. I asked, "Laura, can you think of any reason why you're reluctant to renounce idolatry?" She hemmed and hawed a little and finally said, "Well, maybe because I hang out with my boyfriend's Satanic band. I know it's wrong, but it's the only place where I feel secure and where I have friends."

I explained, "Laura, Jesus is going to be your security. He is going to provide new friends for you. He's going to give you everything you need if you trust him. Can you trust him?" She nodded. Then she was able to renounce idolatry without any hesitation. The spirit of idolatry had just lost its foothold in her, and it had no more grounds to remain. So we commanded it to leave in the name of Jesus. It seemed as if a weight had lifted off her.

But there was more. At this point Laura trusted us enough that she pulled up the sleeve of her shirt and showed us her forearm. Written all over it in ink were Satanic symbols. Thankfully, they were not tattoos. She then pulled a paper out of her pocket, unfolded it, and showed it to us. Written all over it were more

Satanic writings and symbols. She said, "I have a whole stack of notebooks like this at home." I said, "Laura, how about after we finish praying we go to the washroom and you wash all that off your arm and throw the paper away, then when you go home you throw away the notebooks?" She eagerly agreed.

But there was yet another layer to the onion. As we continued to pray, there still seemed to be an obstacle. I asked, "Laura, is there anything else that you think we need to pray about?" She looked down at her feet and said softly, "Masturbation." I said, "Laura, it's really good that you've brought that into the light so the Lord can set you free."

As a non-Catholic, Laura did not have access to the Sacrament of Reconciliation, but I led her in a prayer asking the Lord's forgiveness, renouncing this sin and proclaiming victory over it by the power of his cross and resurrection. If we had been in a Catholic context, I would have urged Laura to avail herself of this sacrament as soon as possible. But the Lord has his own ways of making up for what people lack. Again it seemed as if a weight had lifted off her.

We prayed a little more, asking God to bless her and fill her with his Holy Spirit, and suddenly Laura burst out with a prayer-proclamation of her own. Her words tumbled out so fast the interpreter could barely up with her. She shouted out something like this: "I have been saved and cleansed by the blood of Jesus! I am a daughter of God and he has redeemed me! He has given me his Holy Spirit, and he has given me gifts that I am going to use for his glory! I proclaim the victory of his kingdom! I am going to serve him and evangelize and lead others to him!"

Laura was in effect prophesying over herself, proclaiming in the power of the Holy Spirit her true dignity and destiny as a daughter of God. The Lord had given her a glimpse of the beautiful mission he had for her life. She was transformed!

Afterward we went to the washroom and she washed the dark symbols off her arm. She left the church that night a new person. Although she had only begun a healing journey that will no doubt continue for years, Jesus had set her free. And I realized in a new way the truth of his words, "The Spirit of the Lord is upon me.... He has sent me to proclaim release to the captives,... to set at liberty those who are oppressed" (Luke 4:18).

The Fullness of Healing

How often people come to a healing service or ask for prayer with a limited aim. They just want to have their physical problems dealt with so they can go back to their normal activities and move on with their life. They are not necessarily interested in meeting the Healer himself and receiving the ultimate healing, a relationship with him. The Lord always desires to give us that full healing, but he will never override human freedom. We always remain free to accept or refuse his gentle invitation. Coercion would be contrary to the very nature of God.

The story of Jesus' healing of ten lepers illustrates the mystery of the varied human responses to grace.

> As he entered a village, he was met by ten lepers, who stood at a distance and lifted up their voices and said, "Jesus, Master, have mercy on us." When he saw them he said to them, "Go and show yourselves to the priests." And as they went they were cleansed. Then one of them, seeing that he was healed, turned back, praising God with a loud voice; and he fell on his face at Jesus' feet, giving him thanks. Now he was a Samaritan. Then said Jesus, "Were not ten cleansed? Where are the nine? Was no one found to return and give praise to God except this foreigner?" And he said to him, "Rise and go your way; your faith has made you well." (Luke 17:12–19)

It is not accidental that the ten lepers stood at a distance. On one level, this was simply because the law of Moses required people with skin disease to keep apart from others (Lev 13:45–46). But their physical position also seems to suggest a spiritual distance from Jesus. They are reluctant to come too close to him.

Jesus respected their caution and, without seeking to touch them as he had touched the one leper (Mark 1:40–45), he simply sent them to the priests, those authorized to determine whether skin disease has been cleared up (Lev 14). All ten carried out this act of faith: they set out to have their healings confirmed before the healings had occurred. Somewhere along the way, they found to their amazement that they had in fact been healed! But nine of them simply continued on the way. They showed no particular interest in the one who healed them, no desire to find out who it was who had such life-giving power, not even the common courtesy to thank him.

But one leper "turned back" — a verb that suggests the "turning" of conversion. He gave what Scripture often describes as the right human response to God's mighty deeds: loud praise and thanks, publicizing to everyone within earshot the wonderful things the Lord had done for him.

> I will give thanks to the LORD with my whole heart;
> I will tell of all your wonderful deeds. (Ps 9:1)

> My lips will shout for joy, when I sing praises to you; my soul also, which you have redeemed. (Ps 71:23)

No longer isolated and socially alienated, the healed man has become an evangelist, one who tells others of the wonderful works of God! He is no longer distant from Jesus. He draws near and falls on his face at Jesus' feet — a posture of worship, suggesting that he somehow knows he is in the presence of the Lord, the divine Physician. This man, Luke points out, happens to be a Samaritan. He had therefore been doubly outcast — an unclean leper and a member of a despised people. But now he has been brought into a relationship with Jesus and, by implication, with the disciples who surround him. The shame and loneliness associated with his former condition are gone. His heart is overflowing with gratitude and joy.

Because of this man's free response to Jesus, he received far more than a physical cure. He experienced a profound healing on every level of his being, and even more, in his relationships with others and with God.

The Gospels show again and again this deeper goal of the Lord's miracles of healing. When a woman who had had a hemorrhage for twelve years touched the fringe of his garment and sensed that she was healed, she tried to slip away unnoticed. But Jesus looked around to see who had done it (Mark 5:30). He did not want her to leave with just a physical cure. He wanted her to meet his gaze, to see his look of love and enter into a relationship with him. Realizing she had been discovered, the woman approached and, like the healed leper, fell down before Jesus. She already knew she was healed, but perhaps at a deeper level now, she realized "what had been done to her": divine life and power had flowed into her. Jesus tenderly reassured her, "Daughter, your faith has made you well; go in peace, and be healed of your disease" (Mark 5:34). His gift of peace (in Hebrew, *shalom*) is not only the absence of conflict, but wholeness, well-being, complete harmony with oneself and others. As a friend of mine says, "He more than healed her, he gave her an extreme makeover!"

Bartimaeus too received much more than a physical recovery. When Jesus called him over in response to his cries for mercy, "throwing off his cloak, he sprang up and came to Jesus" (Mark 10:50). To cast off his cloak was symbolic of leaving behind his former life of blindness and beggary and everything that went with it. The New Testament often exhorts us to "put off" or "cast off" the old self — the pre-conversion self, the self before we met Christ — and all the thinking and behaviors that went with it (Rom 13:12; Eph 4:22; Col 3:8–9).

Bartimaeus' sight was restored, but even more, the eyes of his heart were enlightened. He demonstrated the perfect response to a healing: he followed Jesus *on the way* (Mark 10:52), the way of discipleship, a whole new life of following the Master wherever he leads. Bartimaeus' healing is an image of what happens to every Christian at conversion and baptism: our hearts are enlightened and through faith we are enabled to truly "see" what is invisible (Eph 1:18; Heb 11:1). We begin to understand realities of the kingdom that we could not understand before, and we gladly set out with Jesus on the way — the way that sometimes leads to the cross, but ultimately to the Resurrection.

Physical healings, then, are always meant to lead to something much greater. What does this mean concretely for healing ministry? Prayer for healing should never be an isolated event. Whether one-on-one or at a large conference, it should always include an invitation for that deeper healing that comes from an encounter with Jesus. At the same time, there must be a profound respect for each person's freedom. As the Lord never coerces, so we must never coerce or pressure people to respond in a particular way. Some people are not ready to open their hearts to Christ or commit their lives to him. Our part is to give the invitation, and leave the rest up to that person and God. Sometimes a seed we sow will only bear fruit years later.

Transformation on the Inside and Out

Dr. Russell Willemin discovered how the Lord can use a physical healing to bring about a spiritual healing at the deepest level.

Dr. Russell, a chiropractor and happily married father and grandfather, felt that his life was going along fine although he had not practiced his faith in years. That all changed in February 2014, when he was diagnosed with kidney cancer. Two months later, he had surgery to remove his right kidney, but the cancer had already progressed to stage four. It had spread to the lymphatics around his aorta and was inoperable. The oncologist prescribed a very aggressive chemotherapy.

The day before the chemo was to start, Russell decided to attend a healing Mass at a nearby parish that one of his employees had told him about.[151] "That day changed everything for me," he says.

> As Father Mathias started to speak about preparing yourself, he said we had to forgive anyone we were harboring ill will towards for whatever they had done against us. I couldn't believe how freeing that was.
>
> I wanted to spend more time on earth and grow old with my wife and watch my grandkids grow up. I made a covenant with God deep down in my heart to do whatever he asked if he would show mercy to me and allow me to recover. This was totally different from the "deals of the head" I had made before with God. But God had no reason, I thought, to answer my prayer. I had grown pretty far from living in his presence or following his commandments.

During the service Russell began to perspire uncontrollably. By the time he got to the front of the line for healing prayer, he was soaked to the skin from perspiration. He told the prayer minister, Tom Naemi (mentioned in chapter 8 above), that he was asking to be healed of kidney cancer. As Tom put his hands on him and began to pray, Russell fell to the floor. Tom called over several others to help him pray. Russell recalls,

I could hear them all and feel them all, but couldn't move. I don't know how long I lay there. God told me then very clearly that I would recover from cancer, but not without pain and not without consequences for how far I had grown away from him and the extent he had to go to get my attention. When I went to move, I couldn't open my eyes or move my body. My legs were straight, stiff and trembling. So I rested until the spasms and trembling stopped. I decided a second time to get up, and this time my eyes opened and I was able to stand.

For weeks afterward I couldn't explain what happened or discuss it without crying. I told my wife Kathy what God told me when I was on the floor. She asked me if I was still going to do the chemo. I said, "Yes, I am supposed to. I was told I was going to be healed and survive, but that it would not be without pain or without consequence for how far I had grown from God."

The next morning, I started chemo. Within days, the nausea was unbelievable and the constipation was worse. I was miserable, but I realized that I wasn't afraid. I haven't been afraid since I received the Holy Spirit at that healing service. A few weeks into treatment, I developed sores in my mouth that were extremely painful and made eating very difficult. My immune system bottomed out. Pain and consequences, but I'll be okay.

I was raised Catholic and had said the Rosary thousands of times. For the first time in my life, I was praying it. Thoughtfully praying it, with conviction. I can hardly get through the sorrowful mysteries without crying when I realize what Jesus suffered for us. The Our Father is completely different when you live by "Thy will be done on earth" and "as we forgive those who trespass against us." I always used to emphasize "give us this day our daily bread" and "forgive us our trespasses," asking for mine but not willing to carry the other side of the prayer.

The same scriptures I've heard all my life have new meaning to me now. I understand Jesus' parables. I see all of the Bible's relevance to today, to my life. I see that Jesus' words save us. The immeasurable magnitude of God's love for us. The road to life full of peace and joy. And I have no fear. Imagine being able to face life-threatening cancer without fear. It aids your recovery, I'll tell you.

The symptoms I was supposed to have — severe nausea, constipation, mouth sores, a metallic taste to all of food, difficulty eating — I've had none of them after the first cycle. By the end of cycle 3, the CT scan showed the cancer in the lymphatics around my aorta was gone. The doctor was elated and kept talking about how lucky we were the treatment was being so effective. He was surprised by my calm, unexcited demeanor. He didn't realize that by the time of that test, I had known it was gone for three months and had been thanking God every day.

I strive now to stay in God's presence all day every day. I speak out his name all day just to bring my awareness back to HIM. For that, he offers us love, support and forgiveness beyond our comprehension. He gives us the gift of another day on earth with our loved ones.

I went that day for a physical healing.
What I received was definitely a two-for-one; I
also received a spiritual healing.

Russell had simply wanted his cancer to be cured so
he could spend more time on earth. But God had in mind so
much more. He not only healed Russell's body but brought
home a lost son, restoring him to the fullness of life and intimate communion with his heavenly Father.

CHAPTER TWELVE

Three Keys for Seeing the Lord's Power to Heal

Paul looked directly at him, saw that he had faith to be healed, and called out, "Stand up on your feet!" At that, the man jumped up and began to walk.

— Acts 14:9–10

My friend Katie Gesto, a lay missionary and nurse practitioner, was working in a Catholic hospital in the Nuba Mountains, a remote, war-torn area of Sudan. One day in 2011, a ten-year-old boy was carried in, suffering the effects of a venomous snakebite he had received four hours previously. In Katie's words:

> He was comatose and showed all the symptoms of dying from the toxic bite, likely from a cobra or mamba. His lungs were filled with fluid, he had apneic breathing, a thready pulse, and no response to pain. We gave him one antivenom, which was all we had, but he needed five, and we were not even sure if it was the right antivenom. He got worse after the injection.
>
> After the doctor attended to Adam for an hour, I continued to pray over him and told his anxious family members, who were not Christian, to pray to Yesu al-Massih (Jesus the Messiah). I prayed in tongues for him for about

165

an hour, but he didn't improve. I showed them how to care for his limp, non-responsive body by laying him on his side to aid breathing. Late in the evening I went to my house.

At about 3:00 am I woke up and Adam immediately came to mind. I felt a sense of death over him. But faith rose up, and I prayed out loud, "In the name of Jesus, Adam, you will not die, you will live!" I then went back to sleep.

Early in the morning I went to the clinic and there was Adam outside, eating breakfast! He looked up at me as if he recognized me, although he had probably never seen a white person. I called him over as his parents watched with big smiles. I hugged him so tightly. "Yesu al-Massih!" The parents knew it was Jesus who had healed their son. I prayed a blessing over this boy, praying that his life will impact his nation for the gospel of Jesus Christ. He left the hospital changed forever and strong.

Through Katie's kindness and expert medical care this family experienced the love of Christ. Even more, because she prayed for healing and openly proclaimed the name of Jesus, they experienced firsthand the Lord's healing power. The glorious name of Jesus became known among people who had not known it before. A seed of faith was planted in their hearts that may grow over time, and perhaps even lead them one day to the fullness of life in Christ.

What would happen if large numbers of Catholics and other Christians take to heart Jesus' instruction to proclaim the gospel not only in words but in mighty deeds by which God manifests the truth of the words? The New Evangelization would be propelled to a whole new level of dynamism.

For those who desire to take up this challenge, here are three simple keys that will help open us to the Lord's healing power.

1. Intimacy with Jesus

As mentioned in chapter 8, healing is one of the charisms by which the Holy Spirit, the Spirit of the Father and the Son, acts in and through us. The more united we are to the Lord, the more freely he is able to act through us. So the first key to being a conduit of the Lord's healing power is intimacy with him.

When Jesus chose his twelve apostles he revealed the secret of all fruitful ministry. "He appointed twelve, to be with him, and to be sent out to preach and have authority to cast out demons" (Mark 3:14). Notice that the apostles' first and most important duty was simply to "be with him" — to waste time in the presence of Jesus, loving him and being loved by him, learning his ways, letting their hearts become more and more aligned with his. Only then were they "sent out" to preach, heal, and deliver others from evil. It was not a matter of learning from Jesus for three years and then setting off on their own. They had to *remain* close to him, abide in him, return to him again and again to be refreshed in his presence (cf. Mark 6:30–31).

This pattern holds true not only for the apostles but for all Christ's followers. Fruitfulness comes from *being with him* or it will not come at all. Jesus said, "I am the vine, you are the branches. He who abides in me, and I in him, he it is that bears much fruit, for apart from me you can do nothing" (John 15:5). Much fruitlessness and frustration in ministry today comes from thinking (even subconsciously) that in fact we are able to do quite a bit apart from him.

How do we grow in intimacy with Jesus? We read his word daily, especially the Gospels. St. Ignatius of Antioch, on his way to martyrdom in Rome, wrote a letter in which he said,

"I take refuge in the Gospel as the flesh of Christ."[152] The Gospels are the "flesh" of Jesus because they allow us to touch him in a very real way — to get to know his ways, his love, his voice. We come to share in his compassion for fallen humanity, and especially for the poor, the sick, and the suffering. We are freed from all kinds of hidden misconceptions about him that we have picked up from a fallen world. On the other hand, as St. Jerome warned, "Ignorance of the Scriptures is ignorance of Christ."[153] How can we be Christ's presence to others if we do not know him ourselves?

We also get to know him by spending time with him in prayer, adoring him, thanking him, talking with him about our joys and our struggles. We let him warm us in the rays of his love through Eucharistic adoration. We join with others in anointed praise and worship (cf. Ps 33:1–3). When we receive him in Holy Communion, we welcome him into our hearts with hospitality full of reverence and zeal, like that of Abraham when the Lord visited him in the form of three men (Gen 18). We keep our hearts pure by being quick to repent wherever there is sin, and making frequent use of the Sacrament of Reconciliation.

A curious thing happens as we draw closer to the Lord. Instead of becoming more otherworldly or inward-looking, we are propelled *outward*. "The love of Christ compels us, because we are convinced that one has died for all" (2 Cor 5:14). The closer we come to Jesus the more we are filled with God's unconditional love, and the more we long to give it away to the lost and the broken.

2. Ask, Seek, Knock

Jesus made some astounding promises to his disciples, which still hold true for his disciples today.

> "Ask, and it will be given you; seek, and you will
> find; knock, and it will be opened to you. For

every one who asks receives, and he who seeks
finds, and to him who knocks it will be opened.
Or what man of you, if his son asks him for
bread, will give him a stone? Or if he asks for a
fish, will give him a serpent? If you then, who are
evil, know how to give good gifts to your children, how much more will your Father who is in
heaven give good things to those who ask him!"
(Matt 7:7-11)

"Amen, amen, I say to you, whoever believes
in me will do the works that I do, and will do
greater ones than these, because I am going to
the Father. And whatever you ask in my name, I
will do, so that the Father may be glorified in the
Son. If you ask anything in my name, I will do it."
(John 14:12-14; cf. 15:16).

"Until now you have asked nothing in my name;
ask, and you will receive, that your joy may be
full." (John 16:24)

Clearly God wants us to ask for good things in Jesus' name. To
ask in his name does not mean simply to end a prayer with the
words "in Jesus' name, amen," but to ask *on his authority and
in union with him*. The more we do so, the more God displays
the awesome power of Jesus' name before the world. As the
Catechism teaches, "Jesus' Resurrection glorifies the name of
the Savior God, for from that time on it is the name of Jesus
that fully manifests the supreme power of the 'name which is
above every name.' The evil spirits fear his name; in his name
his disciples perform miracles, for the Father grants all they
ask in this name."[154]

St. Paul insisted that there is nothing wrong for asking
for big things from God for the sake of sharing in the Church's
mission to bring God's love to the world. On the contrary, it

is wrong not to ask! "Strive eagerly for the greatest spiritual gifts.... Strive eagerly for the spiritual gifts, above all that you may prophesy" (1 Cor 12:31; 14:1). When it comes to the gifts of the Spirit, God's people have not been asking for too much, but too little. And we have not been expecting too much of God, but too little. "He who did not spare his own Son but gave him up for us all, will he not also give us all things with him?" (Rom 8:32).

What should we ask for? Not only the gift of healing, but all the graces needed to exercise it effectively. Ask that you may decrease and Jesus may increase in you (John 3:30). Ask for simplicity, purity of heart, and boundless confidence in the Lord. Ask every day for a renewed outpouring of the Holy Spirit in your life. Ask for the holy boldness that the early Christians had in proclaiming the name of Jesus and the good news of the gospel, even in the most unlikely or hostile settings. Ask the Lord for a share in his heart of infinite compassion for the lost, the hurting, the lonely, the sick and infirm.

One of the biggest obstacles to being used by God for healing is simply indifference. We may feel some compassion when we see a hurting person or one who has wandered far from God, yet it does not compare to the infinite fire of God's compassion for them. Often it is not enough to move us to take the risk of actually talking about Jesus or praying aloud with the person. The social pressure to keep our faith to ourselves is intense, and hard to resist. It takes a very deliberate decision to cross the threshold, to evangelize and pray with strangers. But once you do, it becomes easier and easier.

A few years ago I came face to face with this obstacle in myself. I was on an airplane taxiing toward the runway for takeoff, when the pilot announced that because of severe weather we would not take off immediately. Nor would we return to the terminal. Because the weather could change quickly, we would have to wait on the tarmac, and the wait might be for a couple of hours. I was sitting next to a young woman who, when she heard this announcement, began to have a panic attack. She told the flight attendants she had claustrophobia and begged them to let her go back to the terminal and get off the plane. They did their best to calm her down, but without success. She was growing more and more panicked, practically writhing in anguish. Sitting next to her I thought to myself, "Poor thing. I'll pray for her."

Immediately in my heart I heard the Holy Spirit say, "That's not good enough."

Oh no, you mean I have to pray *with* her? Aloud? It took several minutes to work up the courage, but finally I hesitantly asked the young woman if she would like me to pray with her. "Yes!" she responded eagerly. I put my hand on her shoulder, commanding the anxiety and panic to leave in the name of Jesus, and asking the Holy Spirit to fill her with his peace. Almost immediately she began to relax, and the panic subsided. She expressed to me her relief and gratitude. Soon afterward the plane took off.

Since then I've been asking God to give me more of his love for people, and more courage in speaking about him. Recently I was again on a plane sitting next to a young woman. This time my attitude was different. She began chatting with me, cheerfully announced that she was a pagan, and told me about all the Egyptian, Greek, and Norse gods she was familiar with and the occult practices she was involved in. Instead of burying myself in a book, I listened, and occasionally broke in with a few words about God's love for her. I asked her whether she was seeking the truth about the meaning of life. She said she was not. After a while she trusted me enough to share other things: the depression and anxiety attacks, the suicidal thoughts, the scary demonic phenomena she had experienced, her parents' divorce when she was little. As she spoke, I could sense the Lord's thirst for her, and I could see the layers of protection she had built around her heart. This time without hesitation I asked if I could pray with her. She agreed, and I prayed for healing of an injury to her knees, and for the depression and anxiety to be lifted from her in the name of Jesus. She did not express any desire to believe in Christ, but I knew I had planted seeds that may one day sprout and grow.

3. "Do Whatever He Tells You"

The most important key to being an instrument of the Lord is given by the person who knew him best, his mother. "Do whatever he tells you" (John 2:5). These words spoken by Mary his mother at the wedding at Cana resound to all Christians of all time. They are in fact the last words she speaks in the Gospels, her last will and testament for her children.

In the context in which these words were spoken, Jesus had as yet done no miracles; his public ministry had not begun. He was present at a wedding and in the midst of the festivities Mary, with her feminine sensitivity, noticed that the wine had run out. She did what she will always do from then on: she brought people's needs to her Son.

But surprisingly, Jesus responded with a rebuff, indicating that the time had not yet come to begin his ministry and set in motion the events that would lead to the cross. "My hour has not yet come." Despite this refusal, Mary turned to the servants with this advice: "Do whatever he tells you." In effect, she forced Jesus' hand! Such was her faith, coming from her intimate knowledge of her Son, that she actually accelerated God's plan.

Just as with the Canaanite woman (Matt 15:28), Jesus found himself unable to resist such faith. Seeing six huge stone jars standing nearby, he told the servants, "Fill the jars with water." We have to realize that from a human point of view, this instruction made no sense. The problem was not a lack of water but a lack of wine. The servants could easily have grumbled or outright refused: "What a ridiculous command." It was no easy job to fill these jars, each holding twenty to thirty gallons. It meant numerous trips out to the village well, hauling up and lugging back heavy bucket loads, again and again. Yet these servants, on the strength of Mary's word, obeyed Jesus and filled the jars to the brim. Their response is a model of prompt and enthusiastic obedience. And it made way for the Lord to work his first miracle.

But before the miracle, another act of obedience was required. Now Jesus asked them to draw out some of the water and bring it to the steward of the feast. Again, this made no sense. Bringing a ladleful of water to a steward stressed out by the lack of wine could lead to embarrassment at best, or even a sharp rebuke. The Gospel does not tell us that the water had already become wine. Rather, the water seems to have become wine at some point *between* their drawing it out and the steward tasting it. A second act of obedient faith made way for the miracle.

How often the Lord tells people to do something that does not make sense in the natural realm, or that is outright impossible. He told the apostles to distribute a few loaves and fish to a crowd of thousands. In the midst of distributing these totally inadequate provisions, they somehow multiplied (Matt 14:19). He told the man with the withered hand to do the one thing he could not do: "Stretch out your hand." And the hand was healed (Luke 6:10). He told the lame man to do the impossible: "Rise, take up your pallet, and walk." And as the man did so, at once he was healed (John 5:8–9).

This kind of radical obedience has also been modeled by the saints through history. At Lourdes in 1858 Our Lady gave a seemingly nonsensical instruction to a young girl named Bernadette: "Go and drink at the spring and wash yourself in it." But there was no spring. So Bernadette in humble obedience bent down and, scraping mud from the ground, spread it on her face and drank of it. The crowd watching her were horrified. Some laughed at her evident insanity, some cried with pity, some were angry. But the spot where Bernadette had scraped mud quickly became a gurgling spring. Pure, fresh water soon began to flow abundantly. A young boy drank of it and was healed of blindness in one eye.[155] Since then countless thousands have been healed through the waters at Lourdes.

How often the Holy Spirit gives us light impressions or promptings that we ignore because they do not seem to make sense or are not according to our plan. To see the Lord's healing power requires listening to him, choosing to be obedient, taking risks, and trusting that he will lead us. Of course it does *not* entail doing anything imprudent or harmful to others. Any inner prompting that seems strange or unhelpful should be submitted to a pastor or spiritual director. But most of the Holy Spirit's promptings are very simple: Go talk to that person. Call that person. Tell that man the Lord loves him and understands the pain he is going through. Ask the lady sitting over there if she would like prayer for anything. Repent of that sin that is blocking the Lord's work in your life.

Even when we make mistakes, the Lord will use them for our humility and growth toward maturity.

CHAPTER THIRTEEN

A Model for Healing Prayer

"As you have believed, let it be done for you." And at
that very hour his servant was healed.

— *Matthew 8:13*

One night while I was on mission in Brazil, our team was doing healing ministry at an inner-city church. A tall teenage boy came up in my line asking for prayer for vision problems. To get a better idea of his trouble, I pointed to a sign on the wall and asked if he could read it. He said yes, he had no problem with distance, but he had a lot of trouble seeing things close up and reading. I asked if he had been to a doctor, and he said no. Once again I was struck by the fact that the Lord most loves to work his miracles among those who lack basic medical care, whose hope is in God alone. Among the poor there is often more openness to God and to the supernatural. Some of this young man's friends were behind him in line, and they did not seem the least bit self-conscious about the fact that they were in church together to get prayer for healing.

My interpreter and I began to pray for the boy, commanding any inflammation to leave his eyes and praying for his vision to be healed in the name of Jesus. After a few minutes, I stopped and asked him if it seemed anything had changed. He looked around and shrugged, "Yeah, maybe." I decided to take a step in faith and asked if anyone nearby had a book he could try reading. After several minutes of looking, someone brought forward one of the tiniest Bibles I had ever seen. It was a complete Bible only a few inches high, with type so small I could barely read it in the darkened church. I hesitantly handed it to the boy, who opened it at random and read fluently right down the page.

"Better?" I asked. All the answer I needed was his big grin. I encouraged him to give praise and thanks to Jesus for his healing.

Although I had been learning about and practicing healing prayer for years, on that two-week trip I learned more than I had in all my previous experience combined. The trip was led by Randy Clark, a Protestant healing evangelist who has a gift for imparting the Holy Spirit to others and who leads several international mission trips a year. These trips, usually to places where there is poverty and great hunger for God, give the team members a chance to grow in faith and in practical experience with healing ministry. My faith and that of the other team members grew exponentially as we saw God's power released in dramatic ways.

Randy uses a five-step model of healing prayer that is simple and effective. This model provides a way to cooperate with the Holy Spirit as he ministers his healing power through us. It is by no means the only way to pray for healing, but it is a good way to get started. The steps below are adapted from that model.[156]

For those interested in learning more, the Charism Schools led by healing evangelist Damian Stayne are an excellent way to learn healing ministry within a Catholic context.[157] Those who are well grounded in the Catholic faith can also benefit enormously from Randy Clark's books, workshops, and mission trips.

Step 1. Interview

Briefly interview the person, as Jesus sometimes did with those he healed (Mark 9:21; 10:51). Ask simple questions in a way that will help put the person at ease. What is your name?

What would you like the Lord to do for you? How long have you had this condition? Do you know what caused it?

In some cases you might want to ask questions that will help pinpoint the root cause. What does the doctor say? Does it run in the family? Do you remember anything that was happening in your life at the time this condition started? The answers to these questions may influence how you pray for the person. If there are no clear answers, simply ask the Holy Spirit to guide you and give you insight.

If the person begins to go into a lengthy description, gently assure him that you don't need to know every detail, since the Lord knows all. Throughout the interaction, let your attitude be tender and loving. Whether the person is healed or not, what is most important is that they experience the Lord's love and compassion through you.

Step 2. Prayer Selection

Discern what kind of prayer is needed. As noted in chapter 3, the apostles sometimes healed by a prayer of petition, but more often by a word of command. Both are effective ways to pray.

A prayer of petition is asking the Lord to heal. "Father, in the name of Jesus let the cartilage in this knee be completely restored." "Jesus, thank you for bearing all our infirmities and carrying our diseases in your own body on the cross. Please free Maggie from all the pain of fibromyalgia." "Holy Spirit, come. Release your power for the healing of Kevin's retina."

A word of command is addressed not to God but to the condition itself. "Ankle bones, be restored and come into proper placement in the name of Jesus." "Arthritis, I command you in the name of Jesus to leave Abby's body right now." "Ears, be opened in the name of Jesus." "Cancerous tumor, I curse you in the name of Jesus and command you to shrink and be flushed out of his body."

If the interview indicated to you that the condition may be related to a painful event in the person's life, as in the story of Anna in chapter 7, it may be appropriate to touch on that event, without going into great detail. If the condition was caused by someone else (for instance, an injury from a car accident) or was related to some offense, ask the person if he has forgiven the one who committed the offense. If not, lead him in a prayer of forgiveness. He may also need to forgive *himself* for what he has done.

If the condition may have been caused by the person's own behavior (for instance, lung cancer due to smoking), tactfully ask, "Could this condition be related to something you've done in your past? Is the Lord is showing you anything that we need to pray about before we go further?" Let them volunteer sin rather than pronounce it. Never accuse, never go digging. If they agree, lead them in a prayer of repentance, asking for God's forgiveness. Recommend the Sacrament of Reconciliation for any serious sin.

Keep all this simple, and do not delve into a person's inner life. Prayer for inner healing and deliverance should only be done by those trained in it, in a setting designed for that purpose where there is sufficient time for in-depth personal ministry.[158]

Step 3. Prayer of Faith

Ask the person if you can place your hand on her shoulder, or on the place that is hurting if appropriate. Let your demeanor be gentle and respectful at all times.

Invite the person not to pray but to just relax and receive, and to let you know if they feel anything happening. There may be a sense of heat, or tingling, or the pain may simply leave, or they may not feel anything at all.

Ask the Holy Spirit to come. Wait on him before continuing. You do not need to pray aloud continuously.

Pray very specifically, with great expectancy and confidence, using either prayers of petition or words of command or both, as the Spirit leads. "Father, in Jesus' name I ask you to relieve the pressure on this spinal cord and let the discs come into right alignment. In the name of Jesus, I command every pinched nerve to be released and soothed. Pain, leave Joe's neck now in the name of Jesus." It is best to leave out the phrase "if it be your will," which can sometimes be a cover for our lack of faith — a kind of safety net in case nothing happens. Pray with great faith, taking for granted that all our prayers depend on God's will.[159]

Pray with your eyes open. Look for cues to what the Holy Spirit is doing in the person. There may be trembling, or tears, or perspiration, or eyelids fluttering. Let the Spirit lead, and continually seek to follow his promptings.

If there seems to be an emotional block to healing, help the person name and renounce spirits that have had a grip on her heart, such as a sense of unworthiness, feelings of rejection, inadequacy, condemnation, fear, or hopelessness. Help her recognize that in Christ she can take authority over these inner strongholds. For instance, "I renounce hopelessness in the name of Jesus."[160]

Step 4. Stop and Re-interview

After a few minutes, stop and ask the person whether they feel anything or whether there is any change or any reduction of pain. Ask questions like, "Can you lift your arm now?" "See if you can read the sign now." If they say it feels better, ask how much better. If there is some improvement, no matter how small, praise and thank God for it. Thanksgiving gives glory to God and builds up our faith. "Thank you, Lord, that the pain has gone from a ten to an eight. Father, we bless you and thank you for what you are doing. Please remove all the pain from his body."

In some cases a condition may be caused by an afflicting spirit. In the Gospels Jesus attributed some, though by no means all, conditions to the work of evil spirits. Satan had bound the woman bent over for eighteen years (Luke 13:16). A deaf and dumb spirit was troubling the epileptic boy (Mark 9:25).[161] If there seems to be no medical explanation for a condition, or the person tells you their pain gets worse when they come to church, or if the pain gets worse when you pray, or moves to another part of the body, these are signs that an afflicting spirit may be involved. Do not be afraid, because you have authority over evil in Jesus' name. "He who is in you is greater than he who is in the world" (1 John 4:4). Simply command the spirit to leave in Jesus' name.

Recently two members of the prayer ministry team at my parish were praying for a woman who had severe back pain. After a few minutes they stopped and asked how she felt. She said her back now felt fine but her elbow was in pain. This gave them a clue that an evil spirit may have been involved. So they prayed again, commanding the afflicting spirit to leave her elbow in the name of Jesus. Then the pain moved to her hand. They prayed again and it was gone.

After briefly praying again ask, "Now, how do you feel?" If the Spirit seems to be doing something, pray again, until they are healed or nothing else happens. Avoid getting stuck. If you do not see anything happening with one person, do not keep praying with them too long, which can be draining both to you and to them.

Step 5. Post-Prayer Suggestion

If the person is healed, rejoice with them and encourage them to give glory to the Lord by telling others about it, as St. Augustine exhorted Innocentia after she was healed of breast cancer. What if the pain has left, but the healing is not yet verified by a doctor? Then the testimony is as simple as, "I was in pain and now I'm not!" Advise the person not to be surprised if they experience doubt or spiritual attack over the coming days. If any symptoms start to reappear, they should stand firm in faith and command them to leave in Jesus' name.

If the person is not healed or only partially healed, encourage them to persevere in asking God for healing, just as the Canaanite woman did (Matt 15:22–28). Remind them that sometimes healing takes time. Never say or give the impression that they were not healed because of a lack of faith. Instead, encourage and build up their faith. Perhaps write down a Scripture passage or two for them to pray and meditate on, to strengthen their confidence in the Lord's love and his desire to heal. Invite them to come back again for prayer ministry at another time.

Instruct the person to continue using their medication even if they believe they have been healed. As Jesus instructed the lepers to have their healing verified by priests who had the authority to do so (Luke 17:14), so healings today should be verified by a doctor before a person makes any decisions about medication. This is especially the case for the healing of conditions like diabetes or heart problems or mental illness, which may not be outwardly observable.

Commonsense Guidelines

If you have never participated in healing prayer ministry before, how can you begin? If you have not done so already, a crucial first step is to deepen your personal relationship with Jesus and receive prayer for an infilling with the Holy Spirit. Many parishes offer a means to do so, such as the Life in the Spirit Seminar, Alpha for Catholics, or Christlife.[162] Then begin to get comfortable with the steps above by using them to pray for friends or family members. Once you are more confident, pray for anyone you encounter who is in need of healing, as the Spirit leads.

All Christians are empowered by Christ to pray for healing for ourselves or others. However, a person should be part of a healing *ministry* only if the ministry is accountable to proper authority (such as the parish priest or the diocesan liaison of the Catholic Charismatic Renewal) and if it provides screening, training, and oversight of the members. In 2000 the Vatican published a document that provides helpful guidelines for prayer ministry in ecclesial settings, especially in relation to the liturgy.[163]

Following are a few practical do's and don'ts for healing prayer ministry in a parish or similar setting.

Best Practices

Keep the focus on Jesus. The best time to offer healing ministry is after Mass or after a time of praise and worship, in which people's hearts and minds are focused on the Lord and their faith is enlivened. If possible, let worship music continue during the ministry time. An atmosphere of prayer and quiet worship will help bring people into an encounter with Jesus.

Pray in pairs whenever possible. Let one person lead the prayer and the other mostly intercede, breaking in if there is a sense from the Holy Spirit about how to pray. Praying in pairs provides greater support, faith, and intercessory power.

Have catchers available in case people fall. Where the Holy Spirit is manifesting his presence and power, it is not uncommon for people to fall under the power of God and remain resting in the Spirit for some time. Don't assume that people cannot be injured if they fall in this way. Make sure there is always someone standing behind the person receiving prayer, ready to help lower them gently to the floor if they fall. It may be helpful for the catcher to lightly touch their back or shoulder to let them know he is there, so they can relax as they receive prayer. If there are no catchers, have the person sit or stand against a chair so they can settle into it. If the person does rest in the Spirit, continue praying for them for a few moments. Encourage them not to get up too quickly but allow the Holy Spirit to continue his healing work.

Remember that you are not able to heal anyone. God is the healer. He is in control. What he expects of you is to love and honor the person before you. The way you minister is crucial. "Let all that you do be done with love" (1 Cor 16:14).

Mistakes to Avoid

Using prayer ministry as a time to give counsel or advice. For some people, this is very hard to resist. You may see clearly that a person's presenting problem (for instance, back pain, or depression, or tension in a relationship) could be mitigated if she does this or that. You may be tempted to say, "I used to have this problem too, and here's what helped me...." As good as this advice may be, prayer ministry is a time to hold your tongue. The person before you is in a very vulnerable position, and you are there to be the Holy Spirit's instrument of healing, not to be a source of human advice. Giving advice could actually get in the Lord's way and be an obstacle to the supernatural encounter he wants to have with this person. However, this principle does not preclude giving a few simple words of encouragement or sharing a Scripture verse or prophetic sense the Spirit has given you, if it is positive and upbuilding.

Getting out of your depth. If you begin to realize the person needs in-depth healing or deliverance ministry that you are not equipped to provide, or for which you are not in the appropriate setting, simply wrap up the prayer with words of love and encouragement. If there is a sound and trustworthy Catholic healing and deliverance ministry in the area, provide a referral to it. If it appears that the person needs professional counseling, ask a discreet question like, "Have you thought of seeing a counselor about this?" In my parish, to keep things as simple as possible in such cases, the healing prayer ministers simply give the person a copy of the parish bulletin and invite them to contact one of the Catholic counselors advertised on the back page.

Laying hands in a way that is distracting or insensitive. Keep your hand in one place; moving it or "massaging" the person can be distracting. Err on the side of caution. Always ask permission.

Saying anything that could cause guilt or condemnation. You are there to minister the Lord's love and consolation, not judgment. Even where it appears that the person's own behavior contributed to their condition, do not blame or accuse them in any way. Again, never give the impression that a person was not healed because of their lack of faith. Instead, "encourage one another and build one another up, just as you are doing" (1 Thess 5:11).

CHAPTER FOURTEEN

Turning the Church Inside-Out

*And the master said to the servant, "Go out to the
highways and hedges, and compel people to come in,
that my house may be filled."*
— Luke 14:23

Randa Malaty, a Coptic Orthodox friend of mine who lives in Ottawa, was having coffee with a friend at Tim Horton's. The friend, Iriny, was fascinated by a video about healing that Randa had posted on Facebook, and wanted to learn more. As they were chatting about it, Randa looked out the window and saw a woman approaching the door with two friends supporting her as she stepped over the curb. Randa, who is an intrepid evangelist, turned to Iriny and said, "Watch this." She tells what happened next:

> The three ladies took a seat at a table just next to us. I gave them a little time to order their food and get settled, then I turned around and said to the lady who was limping, "I noticed you were having trouble walking. What's wrong?" She only spoke French but her friends answered that she had had a stroke and her leg was numb and she couldn't lift it. I asked if I could pray for her.
>
> They gave me an enthusiastic yes and made room for me beside their friend. I put my

hand on her leg and prayed. Then I asked the lady to check her leg. She was starting to have feeling in it. I prayed again and asked her to stand up and check her leg. She got up and started to lift and bend it. She cried out something in French. I looked to her friends and asked, "Is this a good thing?" "Yes," they answered excitedly, "it's a good thing!" The lady's pain and numbness were gone. They were excited and thanked me. We all hugged and I went back to my seat.

Just as I sat down, I noticed a middle aged couple at the table on our other side. They had seen what had just happened and were staring at us. I noticed the lady had a cane on the back of her chair. I asked her if she needed prayer and she said yes. Both Iriny and I joined the couple at their table. I asked the lady what was wrong. She said she her leg was in a lot of pain from fibromyalgia. I prayed for her and her pain immediately left. When Iriny saw this, she burst into tears. She had never seen this before. The lady asked Iriny why she was crying and she replied, "God is so good." The couple were thankful but were concerned that the pain might come back. I told them not to be afraid. They were Catholics so I explained to them that they had authority in Jesus' name and if the pain ever came back to not accept it but tell it to leave in the name of Jesus.

We went back to our table only to see a man sitting by himself at another table. He had witnessed both healings and was looking at us. I asked him, "Do you have any pain in your body?" He answered, "Who doesn't?" Iriny and I joined him at his table. Although he wasn't in pain at that moment, he said he was getting severe cramps in his leg at night. We prayed with him but were not able to verify anything. It turned out he was Moslem and we sat and talked with him about Jesus for an hour.

The best part of this is that Iriny now wanted to learn how to heal. I prayed for her right there at Tim Horton's to be baptized in the Holy Spirit, and when I got home I emailed her some teachings. The next day, she called me to tell me her son's tutor was over and as she was leaving, Iriny noticed she was limping and asked her what was wrong. The tutor's ankle was in pain and swollen from arthritis. Iriny prayed for her and all the pain and the swelling immediately left.

A week later, Iriny called me again, telling me about all the people she prayed for that she had seen healed at the mall. She was discouraged, though, because the last person she prayed for was in a wheelchair and he wasn't healed. Amazing. So far, Iriny had seen everyone she prayed with get healed and she couldn't understand why this man in the wheelchair wasn't. Although he wasn't healed, he was so touched by her love and desire to see him healed that he asked her what church she went to. He took the address and showed up the following Sunday. I encouraged Iriny and told her that sometimes we don't see everyone healed but to never give up. Jesus said if we believe, we will see it, so we need to keep seeking Jesus and growing in our faith.

Because of Randa's courage, healing and evangelization broke out all over Tim Horton's that day, and then spread out in a widening circle. What would the Church look like if large numbers of Catholics began reaching out to others with that kind of faith and boldness?

Going Out to the Periphery

In an interview given just before the conclave that would elect him pope, Cardinal Jorge Bergoglio delivered a message that has become a keynote for his papacy:

> The Church must come out of herself and go toward the periphery. We must avoid the spiritual disease of the self-referential Church: when this happens, the Church itself becomes sick. It's true that when you go out into the street, accidents can happen. But if the Church remains closed in on itself, self-referential, it grows old. And between a Church that goes into the street and gets into an accident and a Church that is sick with self-referentiality, I have no doubts in preferring the former.[164]

This exhortation, which he repeated in his apostolic letter *The Joy of the Gospel* (49), is a prophetic word for the entire Church. The Church in our time, it must be admitted, has in some ways become inward-looking. Catholics — whether in a parish, a diocese, or the universal Church — sometimes look like a circle of people all looking inward and talking to each other about our structures, our programs, our problems, our reforms. Pope Francis is saying that is time for the Church to *turn outward* in a radical way, to go out into the streets, literally, with the good news of Christ.

As archbishop of Buenos Aires, he himself modeled this kind of outward focus. He often took the bus and walked through the slums of Buenos Aires, where he would chat with people, let them take their picture with him, celebrate the Eucharist, perform baptisms and marriages, and manifest Christ's love to the down and out. It is a form of ministry not unlike that of Jesus in the Gospels. Jesus spent much of his time on the wrong side of the tracks. To the scandal of the religious authorities, he was friendly with prostitutes, tax collectors, and sinners — the equivalent of today's drug addicts, ex-cons, and street people. He forgave their sins, healed them physically, emotionally, and spiritually, satisfied their hunger, and caused them to overflow with the joy of the messianic kingdom.

The model for the Church's public ministry, today and in every age, is nothing less than the public ministry of her Lord. So Pope Francis is exhorting the whole Church to radically reorient our focus and go out to meet the lost and the broken in the power of the Holy Spirit.

Losing the In-House Mentality

It is not easy for Catholics to change ways of thinking and acting that have been formed over many centuries. For countless generations, most of the inhabitants of Christendom lived in environments where everyone, except for some pockets of Jews and Moslems, was Christian. There simply were no unbelievers to evangelize, unless one was called to the distant foreign missions. Today the situation is totally different. But the Church, like an ocean liner, turns slowly. Patience is needed, along with fervent zeal.

The in-house mentality is deeply ingrained in us. The life of a typical parish, for example, revolves almost entirely around the sacramental practice and spiritual growth of already-existing members. There is usually some form of generous outreach to the poor, but often it does not include an explicit proclamation of the gospel and invitation to faith in Jesus Christ. Some parishes have begun successful evangelistic efforts; still, many of these involve outreach to lapsed Catholics rather than outreach to *all* the lost sheep, all those who lack a living relationship with the Lord.

I saw an illustration of this in-house mentality when I proposed to a parish administrator an evangelistic healing event, the kind of event designed to bring people into an encounter with Jesus. She was excited and began speaking about how to get flyers for it into the bulletins of all the nearby Catholic parishes. "That's great," I replied. "But that would not be the primary purpose of this event. Flyers in parish bulletins are seen by people who *already* attend Mass. But the very people we want to reach are those who do not attend Mass." "Oh! You mean an ecumenical event?" I could see her thinking about how many flyers it would take to reach the local Protestant churches.

"No, not an ecumenical event. The point is to reach people who *do not know the Lord at all.* And the only way to reach them is by having parishioners personally invite them, one on one. Part of the goal would be to motivate and train parishioners to reach out to their neighbors, friends and coworkers who do not have a close relationship with God, especially those in need of healing, and to provide an event to which they can invite them." It was evident that this was a novel idea to her.

A parish that wants to implement the New Evangelization must gear up to turn inside-out.[165] This requires a series of initiatives like the following, taken step-by-step, accompanied by constant and fervent prayer:

- bringing parishioners themselves into a life-changing encounter with Jesus Christ
- teaching parishioners about the Holy Spirit's charisms and how to use them[166]
- creating a welcoming atmosphere in the parish
- training parishioners to evangelize in the secular sphere
- providing encounter events to which they can invite the people they evangelize, such as a healing service

- providing a follow-up program like Alpha or Christ-Life that presents the basic gospel and brings people into a relationship with Jesus[167]
- eventually, when the newly evangelized are ready, inviting them into the RCIA program[168]

These are steps in courtship — in a love affair with the Lord — and they need to be done in the right order and timing. It will do little good to urge parishioners to evangelize if they themselves have not encountered Jesus in a personal and life-changing way. An encounter event will bear limited fruit if the parish has an unwelcoming atmosphere. To bring an unchurched person straight into RCIA is like throwing a non-swimmer into the deep end. To bring a person to Mass who has little or no religious background is like asking someone to marry on the first date. Sometimes it works, but usually it is far too much, too soon.[169]

Healing on the Street

The unique privilege and role of lay people is to bring Christ into the secular sphere. Lay people live and work among unbelievers, to whom the Lord has sent them. Each of us has been strategically placed by the Lord in particular settings — the home, school, workplace, public square — where he wants to make the kingdom present and draw others to himself through us. St. John Paul II taught, "Each member of the lay faithful [is] entrusted with a unique task which cannot be done by another and which is to be fulfilled for the good of all."[170]

Healing prayer ministry is a simple but extremely effective way to bring people into an encounter with Jesus, the good Shepherd and divine Physician. If such ministry is directed only to those who are already within the four walls of the church, it will soon dry up. If it is directed outward, it will

flourish and deepen in amazing ways. Pope Francis emphasizes:

> We cannot keep ourselves shut up in parishes,
> in our communities, when so many people are
> waiting for the gospel! It is not enough simply to
> open the door in welcome, but we must go out
> through that door to seek and meet the people!
> Let us courageously look to pastoral needs, be-
> ginning on the outskirts, with those who are far-
> thest away, with those who do not usually go to
> church.[171]

My friend Randa, mentioned at the beginning of this
chapter, had another encounter that exemplifies this outward-
looking mindset.

> I was in Brazil as part of a mission team. It was
> our last day in the city of Brasilia and I wanted
> to get a Brazil football shirt for my niece. I went
> with the team to a market and found a shirt.
> The saleslady reached up for a large roll of paper
> mounted on the wall. It is customary to wrap the
> purchase in this paper before putting it in a bag.
> The way she was reaching for the paper seemed
> odd to me, like there was something wrong with
> her arm. As she wrapped the shirt, I noticed the
> muscles in one arm were thick and it was shorter
> than the other. I asked my translator, Suzanna, to
> find out what was wrong.
>   The young salesperson's name was
> Marlucia. She looked about twenty years old.
> "I was born this way," she said. I asked her if we
> could pray for her and told her, "Jesus wants to
> heal you." She replied, "I believe."
>   Suzanna and I took her to the back of
> the market booth and asked Marlucia to hold

both her arms straight out in front of her. She stretched them out and one arm was almost four inches shorter than the other. We supported her arms as she held them out and we commanded the bones, ligaments, and muscles to stretch out and grow in the name of Jesus. We expected to see her arm grow out before our eyes. After two or three minutes we couldn't see any change but she was feeling some tingling in her arm. I figured her arms might be getting tired and told her to put them down and take a break. We continued to pray for a couple more minutes, then I asked her to put her arms out and we would try again.

She stretched her arms out in front of her but as we were about to pray again, we noticed her arms were the same length. When Marlucia saw this, she covered her face with her hands and began to weep. She said, "All my life I have had prejudice because of this!" One of her coworkers heard her crying and peered through an upper rack of shirts asking her if she was okay. Marlucia showed her her arms and the co-worker ran around the racks to us asking if we could pray for her neck and back that were in pain. She was healed, and soon others gathered around to see what was all the commotion. We were running late and had to leave, so we hugged and told them how much Jesus loved them.

Although I had to leave the next morning to go to another town with the team, Suzanna lived in Brasilia and went back the next day to see if Marlucia was there. Suzanna emailed me, "Marlucia was so happy. When she went home last night, her father couldn't stop crying when he saw her arm."

As our culture moves further away from God, it is time for Catholics to awaken to our mandate to be "missionary disciples," availing ourselves of the full supernatural missionary equipment bestowed on us in Christ. Are we willing to lay everything on the altar — the limits we place on what the Lord can ask of us, our sense of inadequacy, our restricted ideas of what God can and cannot do, our fears about how others will react to us? God desires his children to bring his mercy to the world, operating in the full range of charisms and the supernatural power of the Holy Spirit. If we give the Lord permission to do all that he desires to do in us, he will use us to minister his healing power to the sick and the suffering, revealing his love and the presence of his glorious kingdom.

1 See http://www.steubenvilleconferences.com/youth.

2 See Matt 16:3; Luke 12:56; and Vatican Council II, Pastoral Constitution on the Church in the Modern World (*Gaudium et Spes*) 4.

3 Cardinal Wuerl, press conference at the Holy See Press Office, Oct. 8, 2012.

4 Letter on the Society of St. Pius X, March 10, 2009.

5 John Paul II, *The Gospel of Life* (*Evangelium Vitae*) 12.

6 http://www.nydailynews.com/life-style/health/belgian-trans sexual-dies-euthanasia-botched-sex-change-article-1.1473875.

7 Dogmatic Constitution on the Church (*Lumen Gentium*) 17; Decree on the Mission Activity of the Church (*Ad Gentes*) 35–36; Decree on the Apostolate of the Laity (*Apostolicam Actuositatem*) 2.

8 *Evangelization in the Modern World (Evangelii Nuntiandi)* 14.

9 Pope John Paul II first spoke of the New Evangelization as a summons for the Church in an address to Latin American bishops in Port-au-Prince, Haiti, on May 9, 1983, although he had used the term "new evangelization" in an earlier homily in Mogila, Poland (June 9, 1979). He subsequently repeated the call numerous times, especially in his encyclical *Mission of the Redeemer* (1990).

10 *At the Beginning of the New Millennium* 40.

11 *The Joy of the Gospel (Evangelii Gaudium)* 120.

12 Ibid. 28.

13 Ibid. 15.

14 Sociologist Rodney Stark estimates that during these first centuries the number of Christians was growing by as much as 40 percent per decade (*The Rise of Christianity* [HarperSanFrancisco, 1997], 6–7).

15 Paul VI, *Evangelization in the Modern World*, 75. See Avery Cardinal Dulles, "The Charism of the New Evangelizer," in Doris Donnelly (ed.), *Retrieving Charisms for the Twenty-First Century* (Collegeville, MN: Liturgical Press, 1999), 40.

16   Randy Clark is an independent Protestant charismatic healing evangelist, founder and director of Global Awakening: www .globalawakening.com. Damian Stayne is a Catholic lay healing evangelist, founder of the Cor et Lumen Community in Surrey, England: www.coretlumenchristi.org.

17   The passage as Luke quotes it is actually a combination of Isaiah 61:1–2 and Isaiah 58:6 with a few modifications. Jesus is employing the rabbinic practice of combining two related Scripture passages.

18   See Raniero Cantalamessa, *Sober Intoxication of the Spirit*, trans. Marsha Daigle-Williamson (Cincinnati: Servant, 2005), 80.

19   Tertullian, *On Baptism*, 7.1.

20   Matt 9:21–22; Mark 3:4; 5:23, 28, 34; 6:56; 10:52; Luke 6:9; 7:50; 8:36, 48, 50; 17:19; 18:42; John 11:12.

21   Joseph Ratzinger (Pope Benedict XVI), *Jesus of Nazareth*, vol. 1, trans. Adrian J. Walker (New York: Doubleday, 2007), 176, quoting Eugen Biser.

22   Cf. John 10:25, 37–38; 14:10–11.

23   Cf. John 5:16; 7:23; 9:14. Francis MacNutt makes this point in *Healing. Revised and Expanded — The Best-Selling Classic* (Notre Dame, IN: Ave Maria Press, 1999), 73.

24   Exod 7:3; Deut 4:34; 6:22; 7:19; 34:11; Ps 135:9; Jer 32:21.

25   Matt 9:33; 15:31; Mark 5:20; 7:37; Luke 9:43; 11:14; John 9:38.

26   See Congregation for the Doctrine of the Faith, *Instruction on Prayers for Healing* (2000), I.1.

27   For more on these episodes see chapters 6 and 12.

28   Matt 12:9–13; Luke 13:10–17; 14:1–4; John 5:1–9; 9:1–14; Mark 1:21–26.

29   *Against Heresies*, 4.20.7.

30   John Paul II, *On the Christian Meaning of Human Suffering (Salvifici Doloris)* 16–17.

31   In Acts, Philip uses this passage as the starting point for proclaiming the gospel to the Ethiopian eunuch (Acts 8:30–35).

32 The NRSV aptly translates the first part of Isaiah 53:4: "Surely he has borne our infirmities and carried our diseases."

33 Significantly, although Matthew usually uses the Septuagint version when quoting the Old Testament, in this case he provides a more literal translation of the original Hebrew. The Hebrew of Isaiah 53:4 refers to "infirmities and diseases," whereas the Septuagint refers to *sins*: "He bears our sins, and is pained for us." This is the sense in which 1 Pet 2:24 quotes it.

34 Matt 8:15; 9:5–7, 25; Mark 1:31; 3:3; 5:41; 9:27; 10:49.

35 These verses are part of what is called the "Longer Ending" of the Gospel of Mark. They do not appear in the earliest manuscripts of the Gospel, and most scholars hold that they were not written by Mark but were added by a later Christian editor. However, the Church accepts this addendum as part of the canon of inspired Scripture. The Holy Spirit's gift of inspiration is not limited to the original writer, but encompasses each biblical book in its final edited form.

36 See Gaiser, *Healing in the Bible*, 208.

37 Church tradition views the appointment of the Seven in Acts 6 as the origin of the order of deacons. Although Luke does not use the Greek noun for deacon (*diakonos*), he uses the related terms "serve" (*diakoneō*) and "ministry" (*diakonia*) in Acts 6:2, 4.

38 The Gospels frequently mention the crowds who followed Jesus to listen to his teachings or benefit from his miracles; however, there is a sharp distinction between the crowds and the disciples. Disciples are those who have committed their lives to Jesus as Lord (cf. Matt 14:22; Mark 4:10–12; Luke 14:25–33).

39 It is important to keep in mind that signs and wonders are never performed on demand (cf. Matt 12:38–39). Rather, in Acts as in the ministry of Jesus, the miracles are always done in response to sincere requests, or spontaneously at the initiative of the Holy Spirit.

40 The kerygma (from Greek *kerygma*, "message") is the essential content of the gospel, the good news of God's free gift of salvation in Christ.

41 Ignatius, *Letter to the Ephesians*, 7.

42 Origen, *Homilies on the Psalms*, 37.1.1.

43 Cyril of Jerusalem, *Catechetical Lectures*, 10.13; translation adapted from NPNF-II vol. 7.

44 Clement of Alexandria, *Pedagogue*, 1.2.6.

45 Tamburrino, "Healing and the Sacraments," 126.

46 Augustine, *Tractates on the Gospel of John*, 3.3.

47 Ramsay MacMullen, *Christianizing The Roman Empire A.D. 100–400* (New Haven, Connecticut: Yale University Press, 1984), 27–28.

48 Justin Martyr, *Second Apology*, 6.5–6.

49 Origen, *Against Celsus*, 7.4; translation adapted from ANF, vol. 4.

50 Irenaeus, *Against Heresies*, 2.32.4.

51 See Kilian McDonnell, "Evangelization and the Experience of Initiation in the Early Church," in *John Paul II and the New Evangelization: How You Can Bring the Good News to Others*, rev. ed. (Cincinnati: Servant, 2006), 79–93; this article summarizes the more detailed study by Kilian McDonnell and George T. Montague, *Christian Initiation and Baptism in the Holy Spirit: Evidence from the First Eight Centuries*, rev. ed. (Collegeville, Minn.: Liturgical, 1994).

52 *Treatise to Donatus on the Grace of God*, 5, paraphrased by Anne Field in *From Darkness to Light. What It Meant to Become a Christian in the Early Church* (Ann Arbor: Servant, 1978), 191.

53 Hilary, *Tract on the Psalms* 64.14–15; translation from McDonnell and Montague, *Christian Initiation*, 184, 186.

54 Basil, *On the Holy Spirit*, 26.61.

55 *On 2 Thessalonians*, 4. See McDonnell and Montague, *Christian Initiation*, 286–289.

56 John Chrysostom, *On 1 Corinthians*, 29, 36.

57 McDonnell and Montague, *Christian Initiation*, 95. In the Catholic understanding, the practice of infant baptism is essential because it recognizes two indispensable truths: the utter gratuity of God's grace and the intrinsically communal nature of Christian faith (CCC 1250, 1253).

58 McDonnell, "Evangelization," 89–90, quoting John of Apamea, *Dialogues and Treatises*, 10.117.

59   Pope Zepherinus probably condemned the movement in A.D. 200; see McDonnell and Montague, *Christian Initiation*, 119.

60   Irenaeus, *Against Heresies* 3.11.9; cf. McDonnell and Montague, *Christian Initiation*, 120.

61   See Francis MacNutt, *Healing*, 53–59.

62   *On True Religion*, 25.47.

63   *Sermon* 38.2.

64   *The City of God*, XXII.8.

65   *Ecclesiastical History*, IV.27; see also Basil, *On the Holy Spirit*, 74.

66   For instance, Gregory tells of miracles performed by St. Benedict as recounted by four of his disciples (*Dialogues* II, prologue), and of miracles done by St. Augustine of Canterbury and others contributing to the conversion of pagans in Britain (*Letter* 8.29; *Moralia in Job* 27.11.21).

67   Benedicta Ward, *Miracles and the Medieval Mind: Theory, Record and Event, 1000–1215* (Philadelphia: University of Pennsylvania Press, 1987), 1–2.

68   See Ward, *Miracles*; Ronald C. Finucane, *Contested Canonizations: The Last Medieval Saints, 1482–1523* (Washington, D.C.: Catholic University of America Press, 2011) 15–16; Isabel Moreira, *Dreams, Visions, and Spiritual Authority in Merovingian Gaul* (Ithaca: Cornell University, 2000); André Vauchez, *Sainthood in the Later Middle Ages* (Cambridge University Press, 2005).

69   Abbot Haimon of St Pierre-sur-Dives; translation adapted from G. G. Coulton, *Life in the Middle Ages* (New York: MacMillan, 1931), vol. II, 18–22. Coulton comments that "The substantial accuracy of Haimon's description, apart from obvious exaggerations, is proved not only by brief notices under the year 1145 in French and English chronicles, but also by a contemporary letter from Hugh, Archbishop of Rouen, to Thierry, Bishop of Amiens, printed by Mabillon in his *Annales Benedictini*, t. VI, p. 392."

70   An account of Nyla's healing was published in *Legatus Magazine*, "Liberating Freedom," http://www.legatusmagazine.org/liberating-freedom/.

71   Albert-Marie de Monléon, "Healing in the Catholic Charismatic Renewal," in *Prayer for Healing: International Colloquim* (Rome: ICCRS, 2003), 209.

72   Quoted in Eric Metaxas, *Miracles: What They Are, Why They Happen, and How They Can Change Your Life* (New York: Dutton, 2013).

73   As St. Augustine wrote, "God, the Author and Creator of all natures, does nothing contrary to nature.... There is, however, nothing improper in saying that God does a thing contrary to nature when it is contrary to *what we know* of nature. For we give the name 'nature' to the usual common course of nature; and whatever God does contrary to this, we call a prodigy, or a miracle" (*Contra Faustum*, 26.3; emphasis added).

74   Quoted in Metaxas, *Miracles*, 11.

75   See the helpful comments by Metaxas, *Miracles*, 11–21.

76   Jesus gives similar directives to others in Mark 5:43; 7:36; 8:26; Matt 9:30.

77   Rom 5:5; 1 Cor 2:4–5; Gal 3:4–5; 1 Thess 1:5–6.

78   Keener, *Miracles: The Credibility of the New Testament Accounts*, 2 vols. (Grand Rapids: Baker Academic, 2012).

79   Metaxas, *Miracles*.

80   *Chosen to Heal: Gifted Catholics Share Stories of God's Miraculous Healing Power*, 2nd ed. (Immaculate Heart Press, 2014).

81   Randy Clark, *Changed in a Moment* (Mechanicsburg, PA: Global Awakening, 2010).

82   Father Albert J. Hebert, S.M., *Saints Who Raised the Dead: True Stories of 400 Resurrection Miracles* (Charlotte, NC: TAN Books, 1986); Patricia Treece, *Nothing Short of a Miracle: God's Healing Power in Modern Saints* (Manchester, NH: Sophia Institute Press, 2013). For healings done by St. John Paul II during his lifetime, see Pawel Zuchniewicz, *Miracles of John Paul II*, trans. Paul Bulas and Ted Nowak (Catholic Youth Studio — KSM, 2006).

83   Pope Benedict XVI makes this point in *Verbum Domini* 35b.

84   Vatican Council I, *Dei Filius* 3.4.

85 See Yves Congar, "Pneumatology Today," *American Ecclesiastical Review* 167 (1973), 439.

86 The gift of tongues is a kind of non-rational prayer of the heart, a gift of praying and praising God aloud but without intelligible words (1 Cor 12:10; 14:5; cf. Rom 8:26–27).

87 The Greek verb for "make well" is *sōzō*, which, as mentioned on page 30, can also be translated "save" or "heal."

88 Besides the seven instances of the exact phrase, there are also the three variations mentioned here. One other statement of Jesus is also quoted seven times: "Whoever has ears, let him hear" (Matt 11:15; 13:9, 43; Mark 4:9, 23; Luke 8:8; 14:35).

89 In this verse *sōzō* is usually translated "save" rather than "make well" because there is no indication that the woman was healed physically. But since the phrase refers to healing in every other instance, it should be understood that way here as well, in this case referring to an emotional and spiritual healing.

90 Of course there are other Gospel episodes where Jesus takes the initiative to heal, with no mention of the recipient's faith; for instance, the healing of the lame man at the pool of Bethesda in John 5.

91 "The faithful exercise their baptismal priesthood through their participation, each according to his own vocation, in Christ's mission as priest, prophet, and king" (CCC 1546).

92 Cf. John 6:38; 8:28; 12:49; 14:10.

93 CCC 405.

94 Other examples are "You're fired" or "I resign" or "I take you to be my wife."

95 Jesus also mentions sin after his healing of the invalid at the pool of Bethesda: "See, you are well! Sin no more, that nothing worse befall you" (John 5:14). But here too he is not necessarily implying that the man's illness was caused by sin. Rather, the illness should be taken as a warning of the far greater spiritual consequences of continuing in serious sin (cf. Luke 13:1–5). Jesus goes on to speak about the final judgment (John 5:24–30).

96 See John Paul II, *The Christian Meaning of Human Suffering* 15.

97   Cf. Ps 32:3–5; 39:8–12; 107:17. Numerous biblical texts affirm the link between sin and sickness, e.g., Num 12:9–10; Deut 28:28; 2 Chr 26:16–21; 1 Cor 11:28–30; Jas 5:16. As the *Catechism* affirms, "It is the experience of Israel that illness is mysteriously linked to sin and evil" (CCC 1502).

98   See St. Thomas Aquinas' careful distinctions in *Summa Theologica* I-II.87.8, "Whether anyone is punished for another's sin?"

99   The doctrine of original sin presupposes that the effects of sin are passed down from generation to generation (CCC 402–406). St. John Paul II expressed this principle in *Incarnationis mysterium* 11: "Because of the bond which unites us to one another in the Mystical Body, all of us, though not personally responsible and without encroaching on the judgment of God who alone knows every heart, bear the burden of the errors and faults of those who have gone before us."

100   John of the Cross, *The Dark Night of the Soul*, 2.10.1–2.

101   For more on the healing of inner wounds see Bob Schuchts, *Be Healed: A Guide to Encountering the Powerful Love of Jesus in Your Life* (Notre Dame, IN: Ave Maria Press, 2014).

102   Pope Francis, Morning Meditation in the chapel of the Domus Sanctae Marthae (*L'Osservatore Romano*, weekly ed. in English, May 29, 2013).

103   The Life in the Spirit Seminar is a seven-week course designed to lead people into a deeper personal commitment to Jesus and an experience of the Holy Spirit and his gifts. A DVD version is available from Renewal Ministries (see footnote 162).

104   For an explanation of resting in the Spirit, see pp. 139–140 and 182–183.

105   See George Montague, *First Corinthians*, 203, 221.

106   This list comes from the Septuagint version of Isaiah 11:1–3.

107   CCC 1831; cf. Jean Daniélou, *The Bible and the Liturgy* (Notre Dame, IN: University of Notre Dame Press, 1956), 114–126.

108   Paul makes one exception: the gift of tongues as a prayer language, which builds up the person who uses it (1 Cor 14:4).

109   Whereas Paul usually speaks of "charisms," for the gifts described in 1 Cor 12–14 he also uses the term "spiritual gifts" (*pneumatika*, 12:1; 14:1), perhaps because these more obviously supernatural gifts are especially dependent on docility to the Spirit.

110   Francis Xavier, *Letter 14, To the Society at Rome* (1542).

111   CCC 1510.

112   To publicly confess sins is an ancient biblical and Christian tradition: see Lev 16:21; Tob 3:1–6; *Didache* 4.14; 14.1.

113   John Paul II, Address at the World Congress of Ecclesial Movements and New Communities, May 30, 1998.

114   Dogmatic Constitution on the Church (*Lumen Gentium*) 12.

115   Decree on the Apostolate of the Laity (*Apostolicam Actuositatem*) 3; emphasis added.

116   Joseph Ratzinger (Benedict XVI), "The Ecclesial Movements: A Theological Reflection on Their Place in the Church," in *Movements in the Church. Proceedings of the World Congress of the Ecclesial Movements* (Vatican City: Pontificium Consilium pro Laicis, 1999), 23–51. Available at www.stucom.nl/algemeen/alldocnl.htm.

117   John Paul II, *The Lay Members of Christ's Faithdul People (Christifideles Laici)* 24.

118   See Zuchniewicz, *Miracles of John Paul II.*

119   Cf. Acts 14:22; Rom 5:3; 2 Cor 4:17; 2 Thess 1:4–5.

120   John Paul II, *On the Christian Meaning of Human Suffering* 27; emphasis in the original.

121   Matt 5:11; 10:24–25; Luke 6:21–23; 21:12–19; John 15:18–21; 16:33.

122   2 Cor 11:21–28; cf. 1 Cor 4:11–13; 2 Cor 1:5–6; 4:8–11; 2 Tim 3:12.

123   See Congregation for the Doctrine of the Faith, *Instruction on Prayers for Healing,* I.1. Pope John Paul II explains, "suffering cannot be divorced from the sin of the beginnings, from what St. John calls 'the sin of the world' (John 1:29), *from the sinful background* of the personal actions and social processes in human history" (*On the Christian Meaning of Human Suffering* 15; emphasis in the original).

124   Francis MacNutt makes a similar point in *Healing,* 71.

125 Matt 9:30; Mark 7:35; Luke 4:39; 14:4; John 9:10.

126 CCC 1504.

127 CCC 1509; cf. 1 Cor 11:28–30.

128 Matt 9:29; 20:34; Mark 6:5; 7:33; Luke 13:13; John 9:6; see also the disciples' use of oil in Mark 6:13.

129 Tertullian, *The Resurrection of the Flesh* 8; cf. CCC 1015.

130 CCC 1421.

131 CCC 457, 798, 1129.

132 Ignatius of Antioch, *To the Ephesians*, 20.

133 In the Roman Missal there are also numerous post-Communion prayers asking for healing, particularly during Lent, "with this New Testament ambivalence of asking for salvation not only for the soul, and not only for the after-life, but also for the salvation of the body, in the here and now" (de Monléon, "Healing in the Catholic Charismatic Renewal," in *Prayer for Healing*, 207 n. 2). In addition, one of the two options for the silent prayer prayed by the priest before communion is as follows: "May the receiving of your Body and Blood, Lord Jesus Christ, not bring me to judgment and condemnation, but through your loving mercy be for me protection in mind and body and a healing remedy."

134 Liturgy of St. John Chrysostom.

135 CCC 1512.

136 Vatican Council II, *Sacrosanctum Concilium* 73.

137 Cf. CCC 1520.

138 CCC 954–959.

139 A relic is an object such as an article of clothing or a piece of bone from a saint's body, which is kept as a memorial and venerated by the faithful.

140 *The City of God*, XXII.8.

141 The gift of tongues seems to have been common in the patristic era, although it went by another name: jubilation. The Fathers did not refer to jubilation as "speaking in tongues" (*glossolalia*), probably because they thought of "tongues" in the sense of the Pentecost phenomenon of Acts 2, where the tongues were heard as actual human languages rather than non-conceptual speech as in 1 Corinthians 14:2.

For evidence of tongues throughout Church history see Eddie Ensley, *Sounds of Wonder. 20 Centuries of Praying in Tongues and Lively Worship in the Catholic Tradition* (Phoenix, AZ: Tau Publishing, 2013).

142 See Neal Lozano, *Unbound: A Practical Guide to Deliverance* (Grand Rapids: Chosen, 2003).

143 Robin's full story is recounted in her book *I Just Came for Ashes* (Dunphy, 2012).

144 In ancient Jewish and Samaritan society, only a man could initiate a divorce; thus (assuming the five husbands did not all die) this woman has experienced a series of painful rejections.

145 Although seven gods are mentioned in 2 Kings 17, Jewish tradition reckoned them as five, one for each nation (two being accompanied by a consort). See Josephus, *Antiquities*, 9.288. To reinforce the point, John uses the word "husband" precisely five times in this passage (vv. 16–18).

146 See Neal Lozano, *Unbound*; and http://www.heartofthefather.com/.

147 Cf. Matt 4:24; 8:16; 10:1; Mark 1:23–27, 32, 39; 3:11–12; 5:1–20; 7:29–30; 9:25–26; 16:9; Luke 6:17–18; 7:21; 8:2.

148 Mark 3:14–15; 16:17; Luke 10:17–19; Acts 5:16; 8:7; 19:12.

149 CCC 1673; Code of Canon Law, canon 1172.

150 For more on deliverance prayer see Lozano, *Unbound*; and *Resisting the Devil: A Catholic Perspective on Deliverance* (Huntington, IN: Our Sunday Visitor, 2010).

151 Although every Mass is a healing Mass, since the Eucharistic Lord is always present with his healing power, the term "healing Mass" is used to refer to a Mass that draws special attention to the healing dimension of the Eucharist, usually by using readings and prayers related to healing and by offering healing ministry immediately after the Mass.

152 *Letter to the Philadelphians* 5.1.

153 CCC 133, quoting St. Jerome.

154 CCC 434.

155 See René Laurentin, *Bernadette of Lourdes*, trans. John Drury (London: Darton, Longman and Todd, 1979), 58–61.

156   I would like to thank Randy Clark and Global Awakening for their kind permission to adapt this model. See Randy Clark, *Power to Heal: Keys to Activating God's Healing Power in Your Life* (Shippensburg, PA: Destiny Image Publishers, 2015).

157   See http://www.coretlumenchristi.org/calendar.php.

158   The best Catholic resource for healing and deliverance is Neal and Janet Lozano's Unbound Ministry. See Lozano, *Unbound*; and http://www.heartofthefather.com/.

159   See Francis MacNutt, *The Practice of Healing Prayer: A How-To Guide for Catholics* (Frederick, MD: The Word Among Us Press, 2010), 67.

160   These renunciations are rooted in the Church's ancient baptismal liturgy, where candidates are asked, "Do you reject Satan? And all his works? And all his empty promises?" "I do."

161   Some biblical scholars dismiss these Gospel accounts as due to a more primitive mentality that attributed anything not well-understood to supernatural causes. However, the Gospels distinguish between natural illnesses and those attributed to evil spirits. Catholic tradition has always recognized the reality of evil spirits and their power to cause both spiritual and physical afflictions in human life.

162   See https://www.renewalministries.net/?module=Store& event=Details&productID=240; http://christlife.org/; and http://www .alphausa.org/Groups/1000042056/Alpha_Catholic_Context.aspx.

163   Congregation for the Doctrine of the Faith (CDF), *Instruction on Prayers for Healing*. International Catholic Charismatic Renewal Services (ICCRS) later developed *Guidelines on Prayers for Healing* based on the *Instruction*, which were finalized after consultation with the CDF (Rome: ICCRS, 2012). See also the proceedings of a colloquium on healing co-sponsored by the Pontifical Council for the Laity: *Prayer for Healing: International Colloquium* (Rome: ICCRS, 2003).

164   Translated from an interview with Vatican correspondent Andrea Tornielli, *La Stampa*, March 2, 2013, http://www.lastampa .it/2013/03/02/italia/cronache/tentazione-sudamericana-per-il-primo-papa-extraeuropeo-XvX5JzVJsZR6Sf99SmPAQJ/pagina.html. Cardinal

Bergoglio repeated essentially the same message in his homily to the cardinals immediately before the conclave. See Sandro Magister, "The Last Words of Bergoglio Before the Conclave," http://chiesa.espresso.repubblica.it/articolo/1350484?eng=y.

165 Two books that offer very helpful models for making a parish evangelistic are James Mallon, *Divine Renovation: Bringing Your Parish from Maintenance to Mission* (New London, CT: Twenty-Third Publications, 2013); and Michael White and Tom Corcoran, *Rebuilt: Awakening the Faithful, Reaching the Lost, and Making Church Matter* (Notre Dame, IN: Ave Maria Press, 2013).

166 The Catherine of Siena Institute in Colorado Springs provides an excellent resource for parishes with its Called and Gifted Discernment Process: http://wqww.siena.org/.

167 ChristLife and Alpha for Catholics are the best programs of this kind: http://christlife.org/ and http://www.alphausa.org/Groups/1000042056/Alpha_Catholic_Context.aspx.

168 RCIA is the Rite of Christian Initiation of Adults, the process of formation that prepares new believers for baptism in the Catholic Church.

169 As the *Catechism* states, "'The sacred liturgy does not exhaust the entire activity of the Church': it must be preceded by evangelization, faith, and conversion. It can then produce its fruits in the lives of the faithful: new life in the Spirit, involvement in the mission of the Church, and service to her unity" (CCC 1072).

170 *The Lay Members of Christ's Faithful People* 28.

171 Pope Francis, homily in the cathedral at Rio de Janeiro, July 27, 2013.